ORIGAMI ROCKETS

ORIGAMI ROCKETS

Spinners

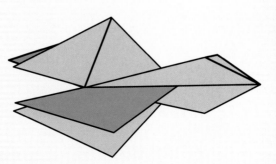

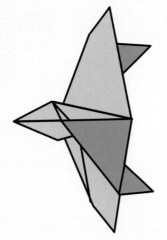

Zoomers

Floaters,

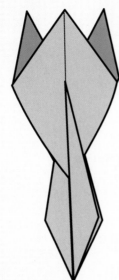

and

More

By
Lew Rozelle

St. Martin's Griffin
New York

Production Editor: David Stanford Burr
Design by Lew Rozelle

Library of Congress Cataloging-in-Publication Data

Rozelle, Lew.
   Origami Rockets : spinners, zoomers, floaters, and more / [Lew Rozelle]. — 1st St. Martin's Griffin ed.
      p.   cm.
   ISBN 0-312-19944-9
   1. Origami.   2. Gliders (Aeronautics) — Models.   I. Title.
TT870.R69 1999
736′.982 — dc21
                                                                98-31678
                                                                CIP

First St. Martin's Griffin Edition: March 1999

10 9 8 7 6 5 4 3 2

Contents

Rockets

Winged Rockets

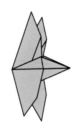   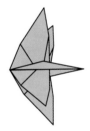

Sweptwing Rockets

Landers

Zoomers

Basic Zoomer 53
Shortnosed Zoomer 55
Longnosed Zoomer 57
Supersonic Zoomer 59

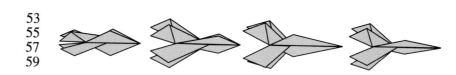

Floaters

Basic Floater 63
Shortnosed Floater 65
Longnosed Floater 67
Supersonic Floater 69

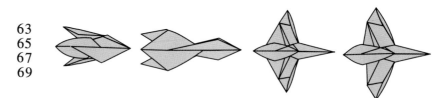

Gliders

Basic Glider 73
Shortnosed Glider 75
Longnosed Glider 77
Supersonic Glider 79

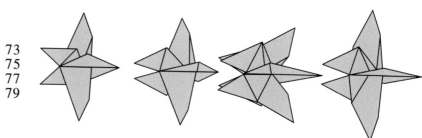

Sweptwing Gliders

Basic Sweptwing Glider 83
Shortnosed Sweptwing Glider 85
Longnosed Sweptwing Glider 87
Supersonic Sweptwing Glider 89

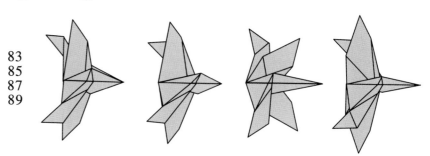

Zoomer Gliders

Basic Zoomer Glider 93
Shortnosed Zoomer Glider 95
Longnosed Zoomer Glider 97
Supersonic Zoomer Glider 99

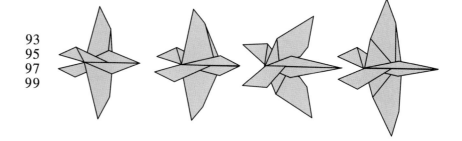

Soarers

Three-Fin Rockets

Composite Rockets

Rocket Designs and Flying

Introduction

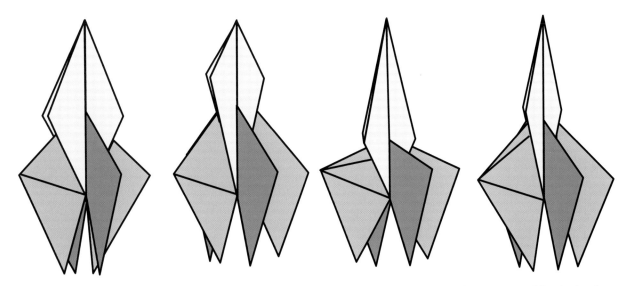

This book of folded paper rockets is an attempt to demonstrate the creative power of logic in the development of an origami idea. A single geometrical configuration, the Waterbomb Base, yields four rockets fundamentally alike but different in appearance and in structural detail: one has a large fuselage, one has a short nose, one a long nose, and one has the narrow fuselage of a supersonic craft.

These four rockets are then refolded with many variations in fin design. Each model can be inflated to produce a rounded aerodynamic fuselage. The resulting rockets not only look realistic but will fly when thrown or tossed: some zoom swiftly to their goals, while others sail, glide, soar, or catch the air like parachutes. An optional Nose Cone adds speed and distance to the flight by altering the distribution of weight.

The type and weight of the paper you use to fold these rockets will depend on what size rocket you are going to fold. As a general rule you will need to use a lightweight paper, such as origami or foil-backed paper for the Longnosed and Supersonic Rockets. These require more folds and a heavy paper becomes difficult to fold. The Basic and Shortnosed Rockets can be folded from a heavier paper such as bond or butcher paper. You will need to experiment a little to decide which paper you like best when folding the rockets.

Although it is possible to start anywhere. There are two principal routes through this book: you can fold straight through from beginning to end, or you may want to fold all the versions of the Basic Rocket, then all the versions of the Shortnosed Rocket, and so on. It will in any case be helpful to keep nearby a folded example of each of the four fundamental designs presented in the initial Rockets chapter.

Application of these principles of variation will help you to create your own origami designs. I hope you enjoy folding these paper rockets as much as I have.

Lew Rozelle

Procedures

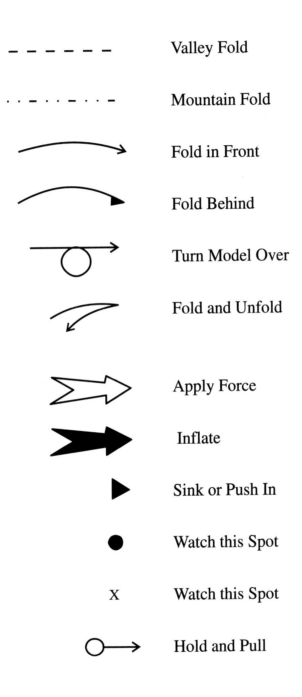

– – – – – – –	Valley Fold
· · – · – · · –	Mountain Fold
⟶	Fold in Front
⟶	Fold Behind
⊙⟶	Turn Model Over
↙	Fold and Unfold
⇨	Apply Force
⮞	Inflate
▶	Sink or Push In
●	Watch this Spot
X	Watch this Spot
○⟶	Hold and Pull

International symbols for folding paper

Reverse Fold

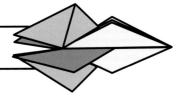

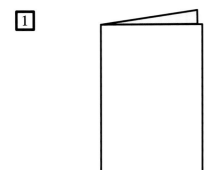

1

Begin with a square folded in half. Push the lower left corner toward the right so that it lies between the front and back flaps.

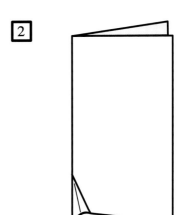

2

Flatten the model so that the large front and back flaps are together.

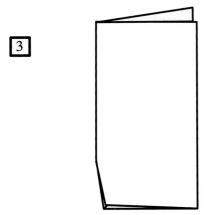

3

This procedure is called a <u>reverse</u> <u>fold</u> because a mountain fold—the left edge in this instance—is reversed to become a valley fold.

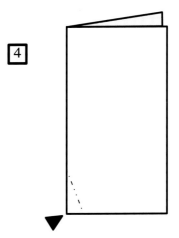

4

The reverse fold is notated like this.

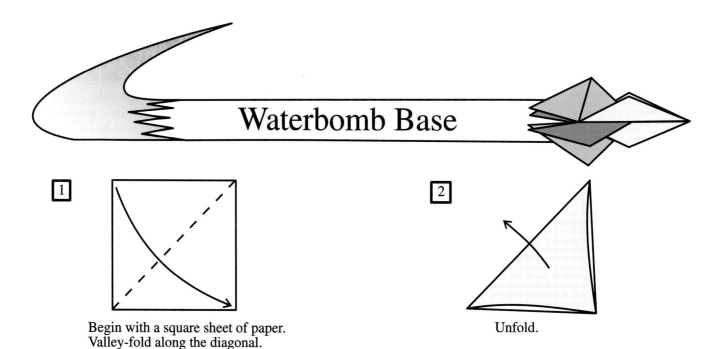

Waterbomb Base

1

Begin with a square sheet of paper.
Valley-fold along the diagonal.

2

Unfold.

The drawings above show how to fold a Waterbomb Base. Begin with a square piece of paper colored side down. Step 1 tells you to valley-fold the paper on the diagonal and shows the direction to make the fold. It is very important when folding the Waterbomb Base to be as precise as you can. The edges of the paper must be lined up exactly. Step 2 shows what the paper looks like when you begin to make the crease. It also tells you to unfold the near flap, returning the paper to its original position.

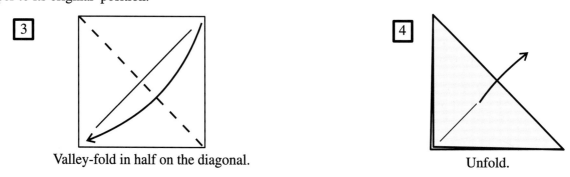

3

Valley-fold in half on the diagonal.

4

Unfold.

Step 3 tells you to make another valley fold and the direction to fold. Step 4 shows the paper after the fold and tells you to unfold the paper again. In later drawings, these two steps of folding and unfolding are included in one step.

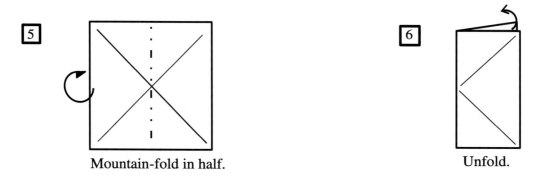

5

Mountain-fold in half.

6

Unfold.

Steps 5 and 6 tell you to make a mountain fold, show the direction of the motion, and show how to unfold the paper. Notice that when you unfold the paper there is no color.

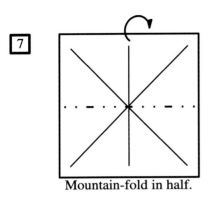 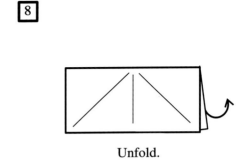

Mountain-fold in half.

Unfold.

Steps 7 and 8 tell you to make a mountain fold, show the direction of the motion, and show how to unfold the paper. Notice that when you unfold the paper there is no color.

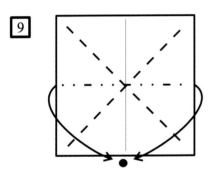 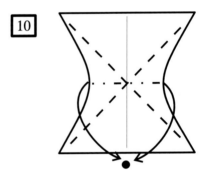

Press down on the center of the paper, then pull the ends of the mountain crease down toward the black dot.

Continue to pull the ends of the mountain crease down toward the black dot.

Step 9 shows all the folds you have made in steps 1–8 and shows how to pull the left and right edges of the paper downward and together to form a completed Waterbomb Base. Steps 10–12 show this process in progress.

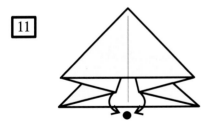 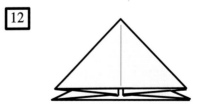

Continue to pull the tips of the mountain crease down toward the black dot. Flatten the paper.

A completed Waterbomb Base.

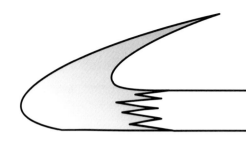

Rocket Base

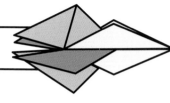

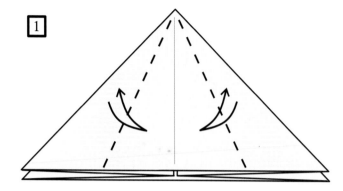

1

Begin with a Waterbomb Base (page 4). Valley-fold to the centerline the near left and right folded edges and unfold. Repeat behind.

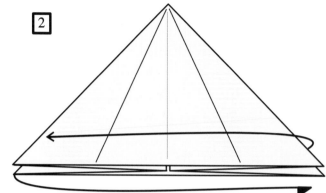

2

Valley-fold the near right flap to the left along the centerline as if turning the page of a book.
Turn over and repeat behind.

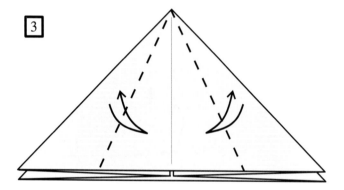

3

Valley-fold to the centerline the near left and right folded edges and unfold. Repeat behind.

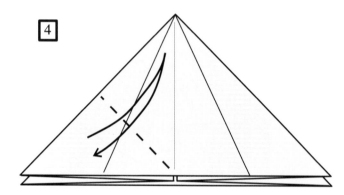

4

Valley-fold the tip of the near left flap up to the top and unfold.

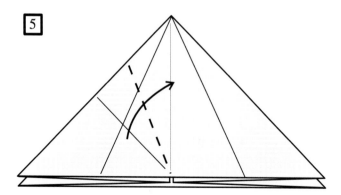

5

Valley-fold the near left flap so that the crease formed in step 4 lies along the vertical centerline and unfold.
Repeat steps 4 and 5 on the three remaining sides.

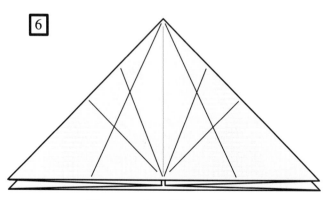

6

The completed Rocket Base.

Rockets

Basic Rocket

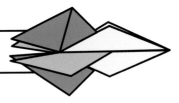

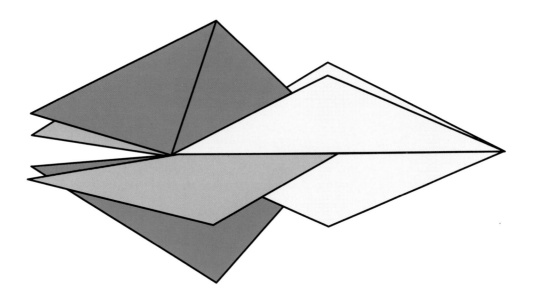

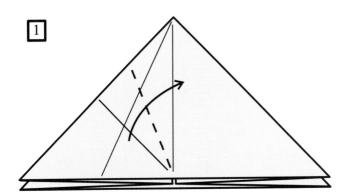

1

Begin with a Rocket Base (page 6).
Valley-fold the near left flap along the existing
crease formed in step 5 of the Rocket Base.

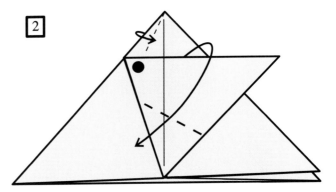

2

Pull the long upper edge of the near flap downward.
The crease already exists, but it must be turned into a
valley fold. At the same time bring the short upper left
edge to the vertical centerline. Watch the black dot.

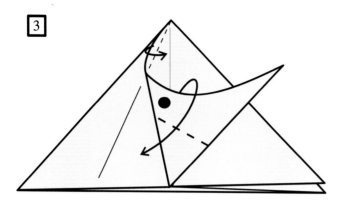

3

The actions of step 2 are shown here in progress.
The top of the left edge will be drawn rightward
to the centerline. Flatten the model.

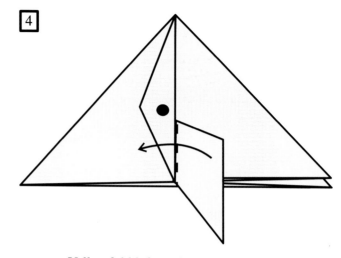

4

Valley-fold leftward the right half
of the near flap to form a fin. Repeat
steps 1–4 on the remaining three sides.

5

!!! CAUTION !!!
DON'T POKE YOUR EYE!

6

The completed Basic Rocket

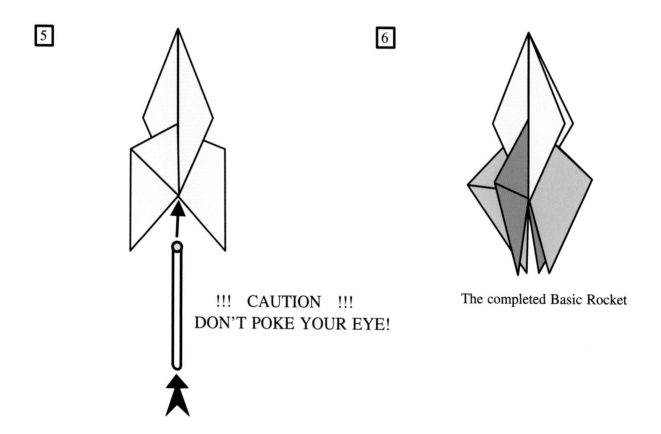

Since the rockets have fins which extend over the holes at their base, a straw may be used to aid in expanding the models. Carefully insert one end of a small straw into the hole in the base of the model and gently blow air into the paper until the model expands. If you blow too hard the model will blow out of shape. You can also inflate the rockets by temporarily bending the fins outward away from your eyes, grasping opposite fins, and blowing into the hole.

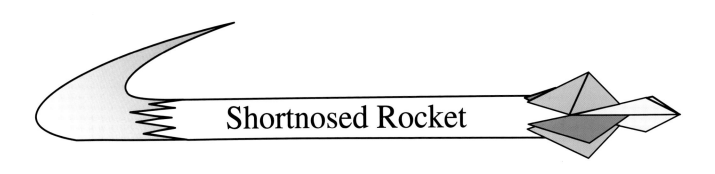

Shortnosed Rocket

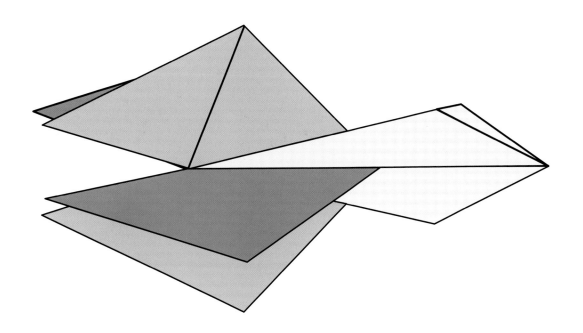

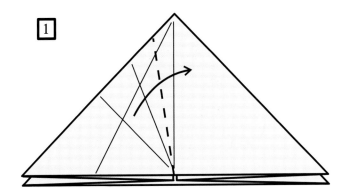

1

Begin with a Rocket Base (page 6).
Valley-fold the near left flap so that the crease formed in step 5 of the Rocket Base lies along the vertical centerline.

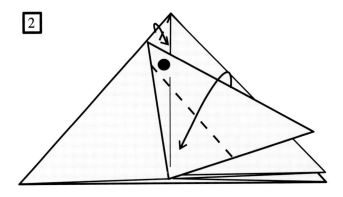

2

Pull the long upper edge of the near flap downward. The crease already exists, but it must be turned into a valley fold. At the same time bring the short upper left edge to the vertical centerline. Watch the black dot.

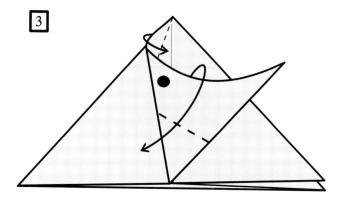

The actions of step 2 are shown here in progress.
The top of the left edge will be drawn rightward
to the centerline. Flatten the model.

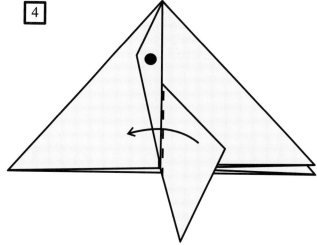

Valley-fold leftward the right half
of the near flap to form a fin. Repeat
steps 1–4 on the three remaining sides.

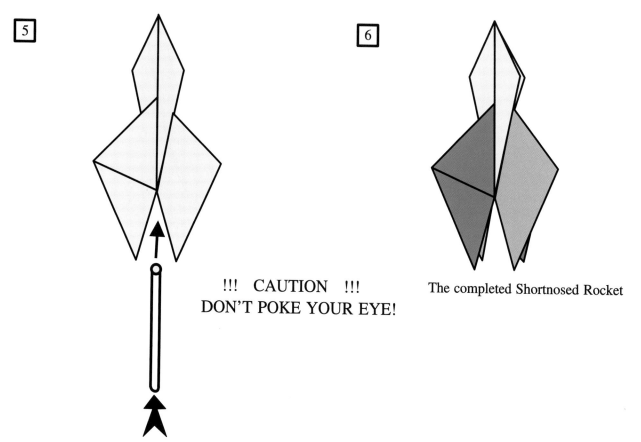

!!! CAUTION !!!
DON'T POKE YOUR EYE!

The completed Shortnosed Rocket

Since the rockets have fins which extend over the holes at their base, a straw may be used to aid in expanding the models. Carefully insert one end of a small straw into the hole in the base of the model and gently blow air into the paper until the model expands. If you blow too hard the model will blow out of shape. You can also inflate the rockets by temporarily bending the fins outward away from your eyes, grasping opposite fins, and blowing into the hole.

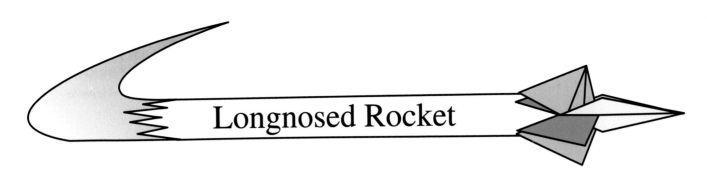

Longnosed Rocket

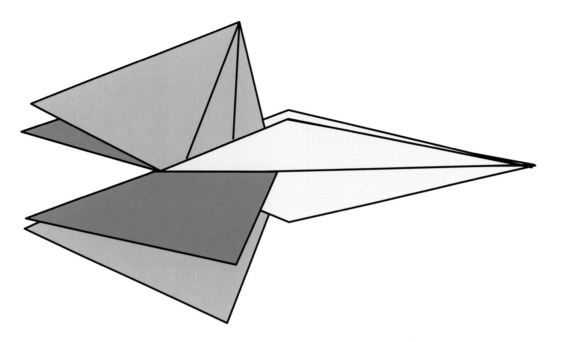

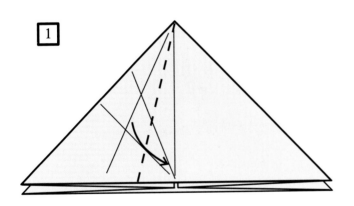

1

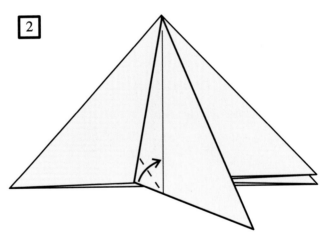

2

Begin with a Rocket Base (page 6).
Valley-fold so that the crease formed in step 1 of the Rocket Base lies along the vertical centerline. The flap will cover the centerline, so you will need to check the alignment of the creases by looking at the far side.

Valley-fold the near left corner to the vertical centerline. The bottom of this small crease must touch the bottom of the centerline; it is important that it should not lie any farther to the right.

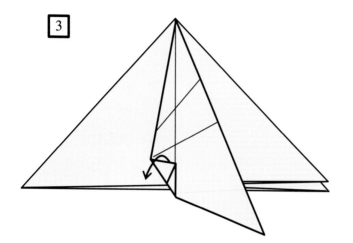

3

Unfold the small corner.

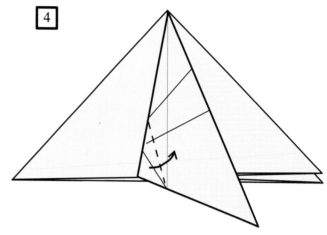

4

Valley-fold the near left corner so that the crease formed in step 2 lies along the vertical crease. The bottom of this small crease must touch the bottom of the centerline; it is important that it should not lie any farther to the right.

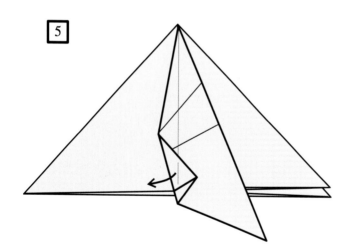

5

Crease very sharply and unfold the small corner.

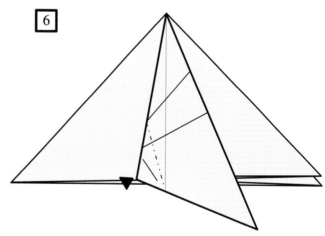

6

Reverse-fold into the model the near lower left corner, using the crease formed in step 4. The bottom of this reverse fold must touch the bottom of the centerline; it is important that it should not lie any farther to the right.

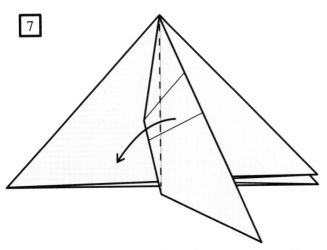

7

Valley-fold the near flap leftward along the centerline.

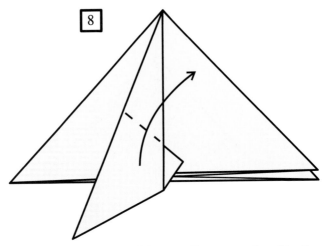

8

Valley-fold the bottom of the near flap upward and to the right in a hinge action. Flatten the model.

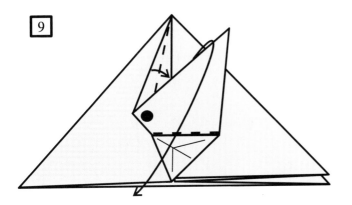

9

Pull the long upper edge of the near flap downward, forming a new crease along the internal folded edge, while at the same time you bring the shorter left edge to the vertical centerline. Look ahead to steps 10 and 11. Watch the black dot.

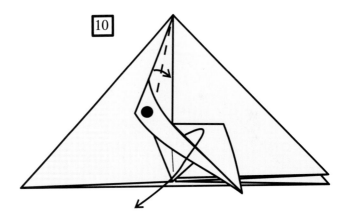

10

The actions of step 9 are shown here in progress. Flatten the model.

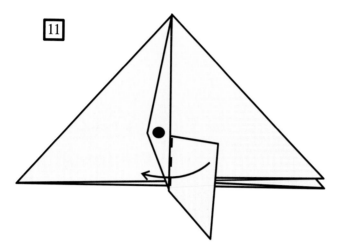

11

Valley-fold the right half of the near flap leftward over the centerline to form a fin. Repeat steps 1–11 on the three remaining sides of the Rocket Base.

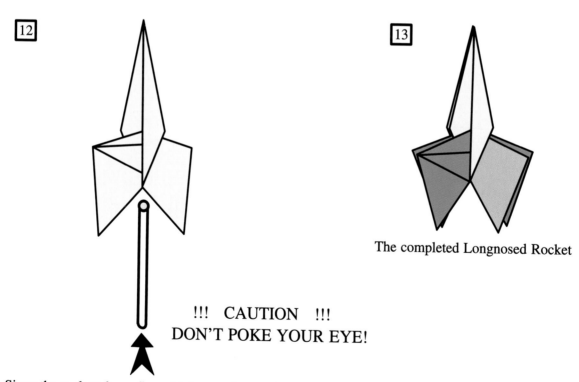

12

13

The completed Longnosed Rocket

!!! CAUTION !!!
DON'T POKE YOUR EYE!

Since the rockets have fins which extend over the holes at their base, a straw may be used to aid in expanding the models. Carefully insert one end of a small straw into the hole in the base of the model and gently blow air into the paper until the model expands. If you blow too hard the model will blow out of shape. You can also inflate the rockets by temporarily bending the fins outward away from your eyes, grasping opposite fins, and blowing into the hole.

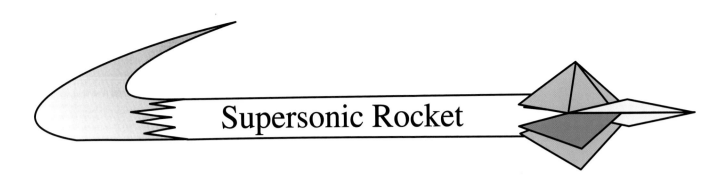

Supersonic Rocket

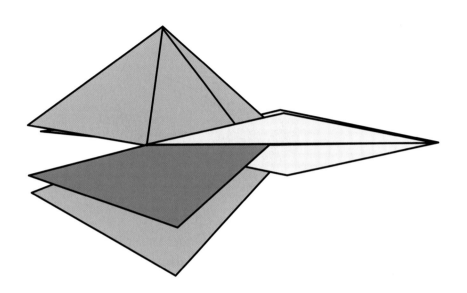

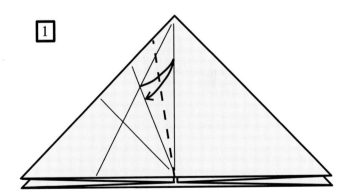

1

Begin with a Rocket Base (page 6). Valley-fold the near left flap so that the crease formed in step 5 of the Rocket Base lies along the vertical centerline and unfold.

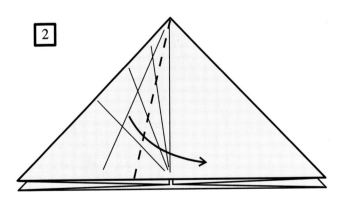

2

Valley-fold so that the crease formed in step 1 of the Rocket Base lies along the vertical centerline. The flap will cover the centerline, so you will need to check the alignment of the creases by looking at the far side.

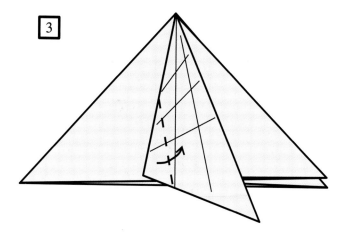

3

Valley-fold the lower left corner of the near flap: each end of this new valley fold touches the tip of an existing crease. The bottom of this small crease must touch the bottom of the centerline; it is important that it should not lie any farther to the right.

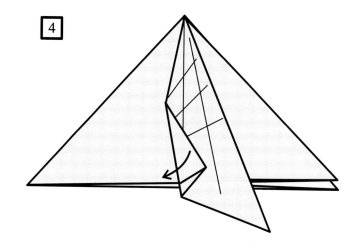

4

Crease very sharply and unfold the corner.

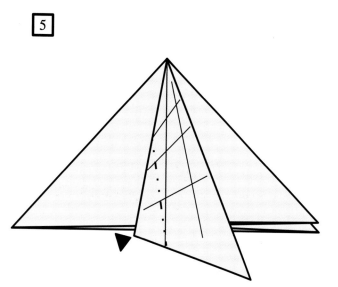

5

Using the crease formed in step 3, reverse-fold into the model the lower left corner of the near flap. The bottom of this reverse fold must touch the bottom of the centerline; it is important that it should not lie any farther to the right.

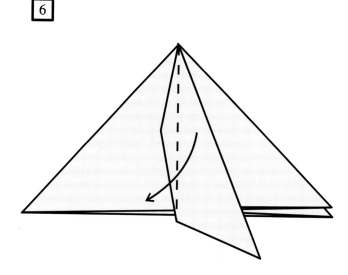

6

Valley-fold the near flap leftward along the centerline.

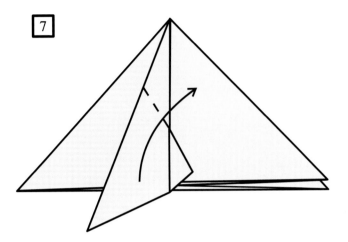

7

Lift the entire near flap and flatten it upward and to the right in a hinge action, forming the valley fold automatically.

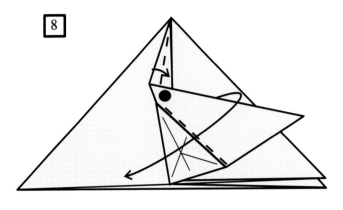

8

Pull downward the long upper edge of the near flap forming a new valley fold along the internal folded edge; at the same time bring the small left edge to the vertical centerline. Look ahead to the next two drawings, and watch the black dot. Flatten the model.

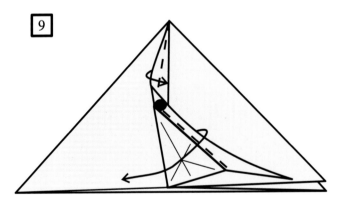

9

The actions of step 8 are shown here in progress. Flatten the model.

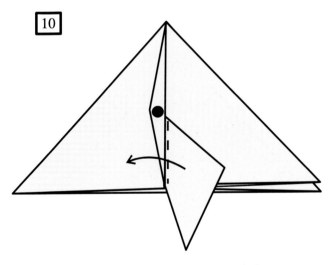

10

Valley-fold the near flap leftward along the centerline to form a fin. Repeat steps 1–10 on the three remaining sides.

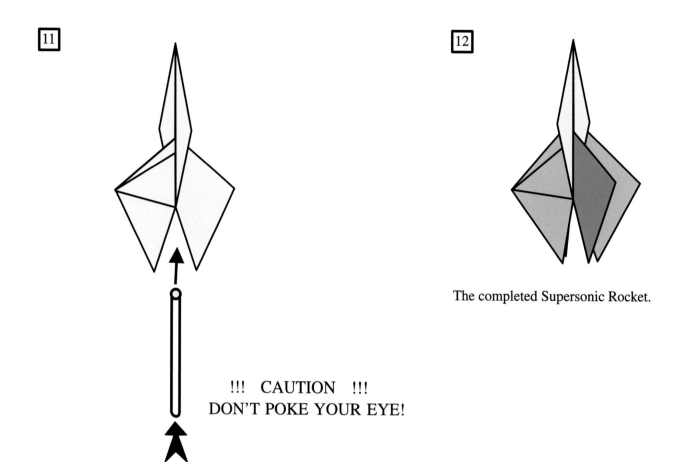

The completed Supersonic Rocket.

!!!   CAUTION   !!!
DON'T POKE YOUR EYE!

Since the rockets have fins which extend over the holes at their base, a straw may be used to aid in expanding the models. Carefully insert one end of a small straw into the hole in the base of the model and gently blow air into the paper until the model expands. If you blow too hard the model will blow out of shape. You can also inflate the rockets by temporarily bending the fins outward away from your eyes, grasping opposite fins, and blowing into the hole.

Winged Rockets

 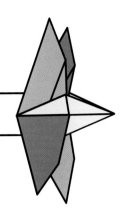

Basic Winged Rocket

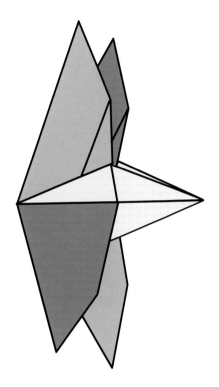

1

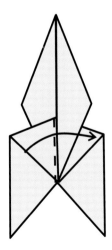

Begin with an uninflated Basic Rocket (page 9).
Swing the near left fin all the way to the
right. Flatten the model.

2

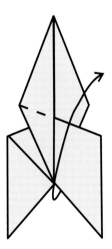

Lift the nearest fin upward as
far as it will go. Flatten the model.

3

Valley-fold the near flap back
to the left along the centerline.

4

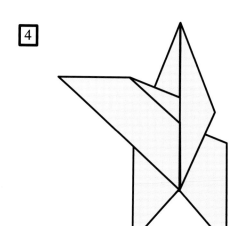

Repeat steps 1–3 on the three
remaining sides of the Basic Rocket.

5

6

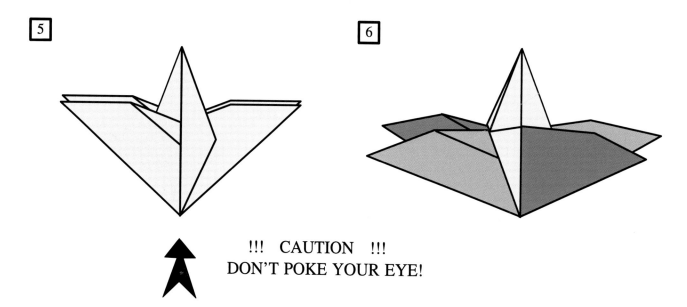

!!! CAUTION !!!
DON'T POKE YOUR EYE!

Grasp opposite fins and inflate the
rocket by blowing into the hole
in the bottom.

Shortnosed Winged Rocket

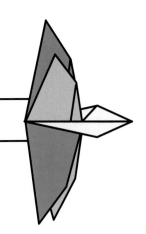

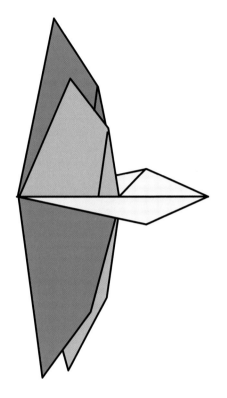

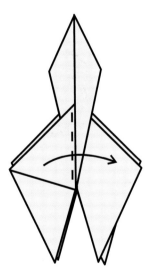

Begin with an uninflated Shortnosed Rocket (page 11). Swing the near left fin all the way over to the right. Flatten the model.

Lift the nearest fin up and flatten it to the right as far as it will go.

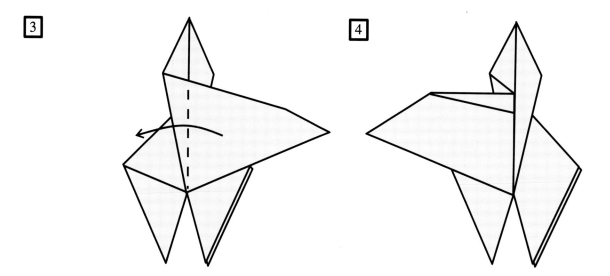

3

Valley-fold the near flap back to the
left along the centerline.

4

Repeat steps 1–3 on each of the
remaining three sides.

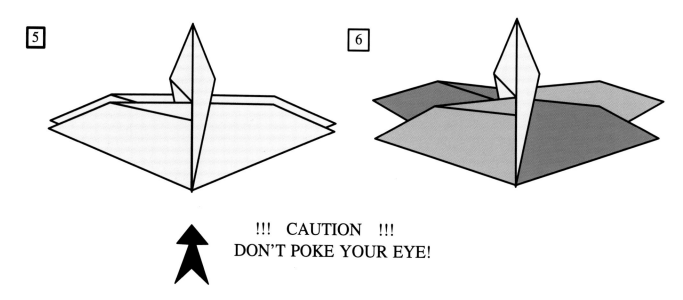

5

6

!!! CAUTION !!!
DON'T POKE YOUR EYE!

Grasp opposite fins and inflate the rocket
by blowing into the hole in the bottom.

Longnosed Winged Rocket

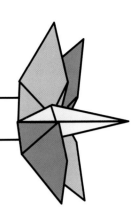

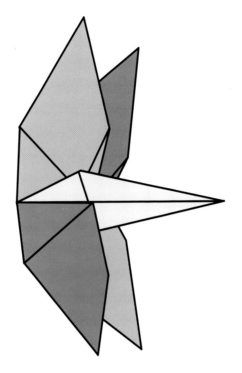

1

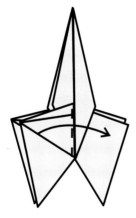

Begin with an uninflated Longnosed Rocket (page 13). Swing the near left fin all the way over to the right. Flatten the model.

2

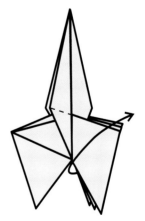

Lift the nearest fin upward as far as it will go. Flatten the model.

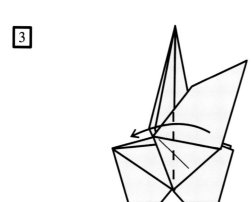

3

4

Valley-fold the near flap back
to the left along the centerline.

Repeat steps 1–3 on each of the three
remaining sides.

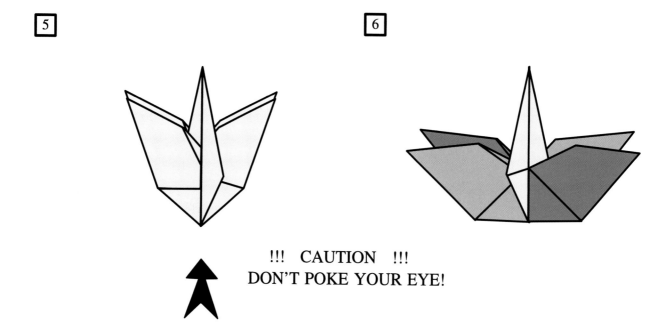

5

6

!!! CAUTION !!!
DON'T POKE YOUR EYE!

Grasp opposite fins and inflate the rocket
by blowing into the hole in the bottom.

Supersonic Winged Rocket

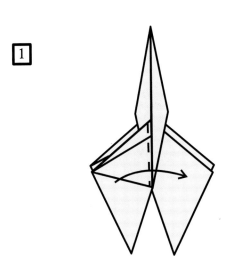

1

Begin with an uninflated Supersonic Rocket (page 17).
Swing the near left fin all the way to the right.
Flatten the model.

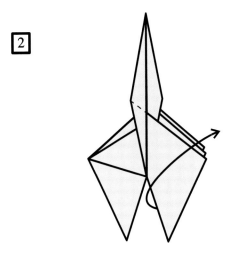

2

Lift the nearest fin upward as far as it will go.
Flatten the model.

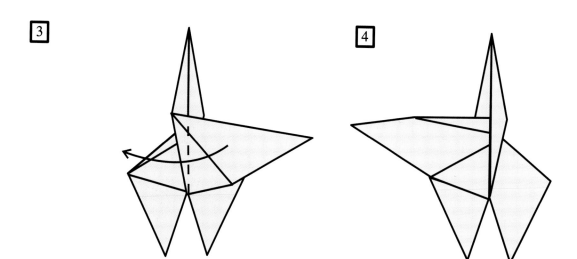

Valley-fold the near flap back to the left
along the centerline.

Repeat steps 1–3 on the three remaining sides.

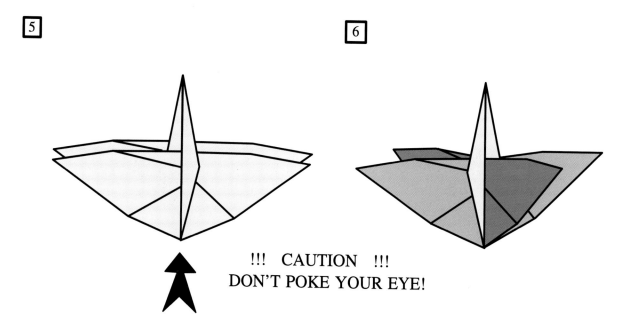

!!!   CAUTION   !!!
DON'T POKE YOUR EYE!

Grasp opposite fins and inflate
the rocket by blowing into
the hole in the bottom.

Sweptwing Rockets

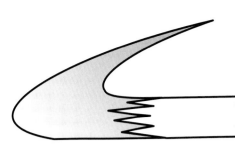

Basic Sweptwing

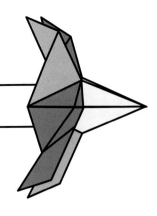

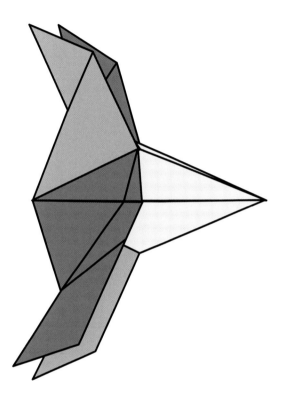

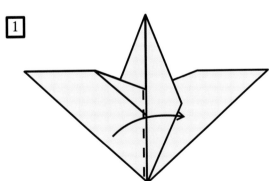

1

Begin with an uninflated Basic Winged Rocket (page 23). Swing the near left wing all the way over to the right. Flatten the model.

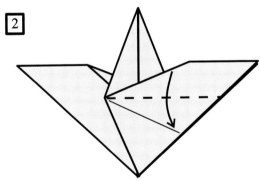

2

Valley-fold the top portion of the near wing down as shown. The new crease should be horizontal.

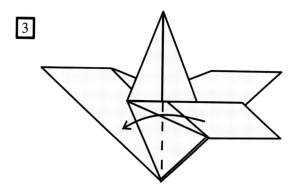

3

Valley-fold the near wing back
to the left along the centerline.

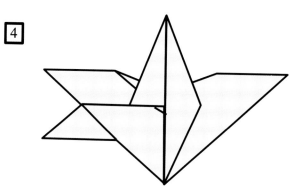

4

Repeat steps 1–3 on the
three remaining sides.

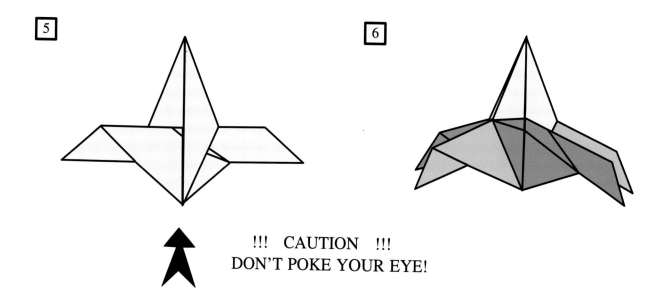

5

Grasp opposite fins and inflate
the rocket by blowing into the
hole in the bottom.

!!! CAUTION !!!
DON'T POKE YOUR EYE!

6

Shortnosed Sweptwing

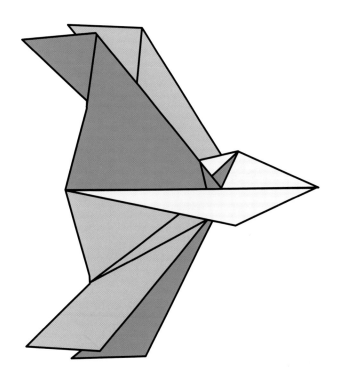

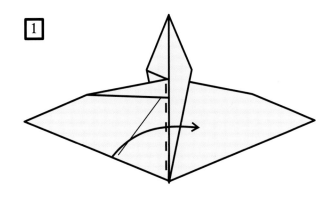

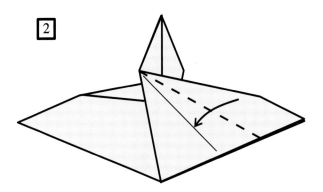

Begin with an uninflated Shortnosed Winged Rocket (page 25).
Swing the nearest wing to the right as far as it will go.
Flatten the model.

Valley-fold the top edge of the nearest flap down to the existing crease.

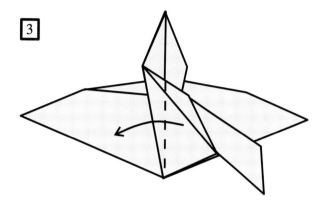

3

Valley-fold the near flap back to
the left along the centerline.

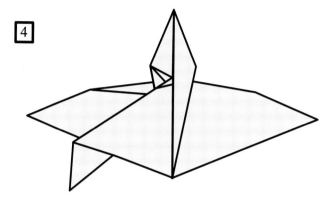

4

Repeat steps 1–3 on the three remaining flaps.

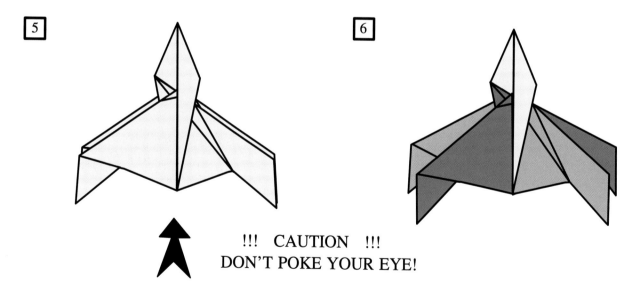

5

6

!!!   CAUTION   !!!
DON'T POKE YOUR EYE!

Grasp opposite fins and inflate the rocket
by blowing into the hole in the bottom.

Longnosed Sweptwing

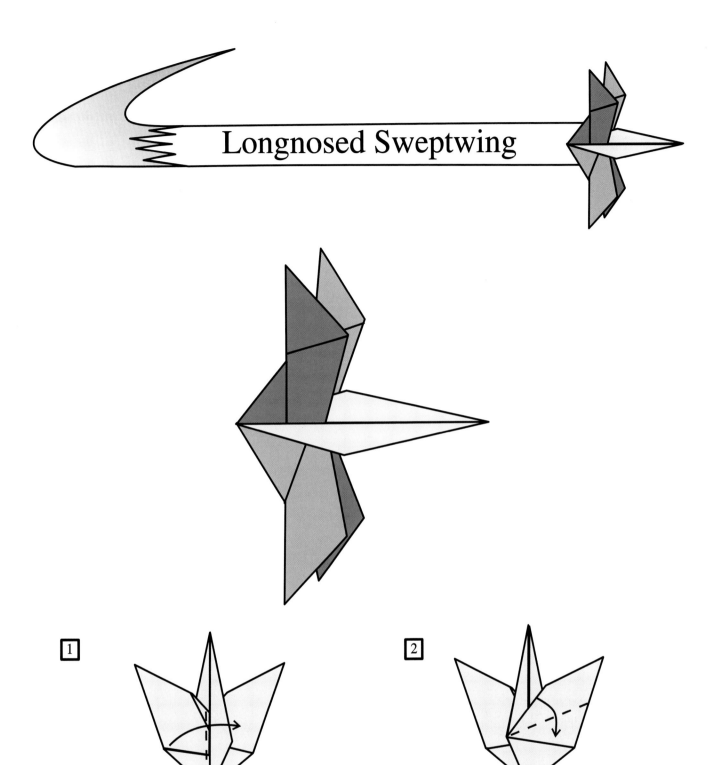

1

Begin with an uninflated Longnosed Winged Rocket (page 27). Swing the near left wing all the way over to the right. Flatten the model.

2

Valley-fold the top left edge of the near flap down to the internal folded edge.

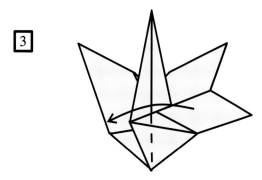

3

Valley-fold the near flap back along the centerline.

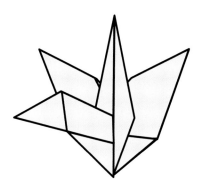

4

Repeat steps 1–3 on the three remaining flaps.

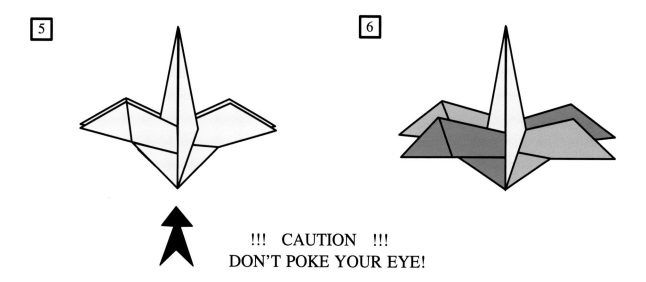

5

6

!!! CAUTION !!!
DON'T POKE YOUR EYE!

Grasp opposite fins and inflate the rocket by blowing into the hole in the bottom.

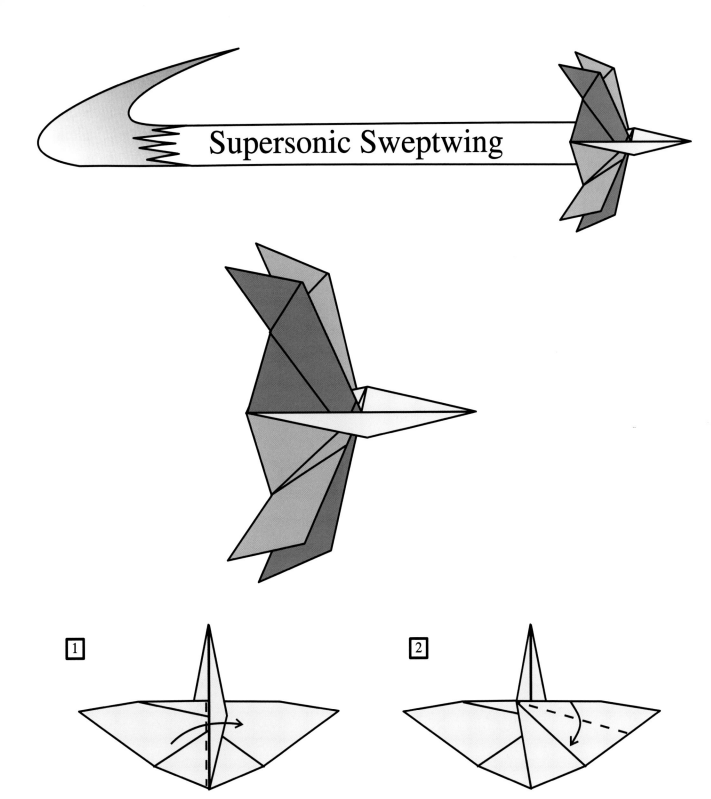

Supersonic Sweptwing

1

Begin with an uninflated Supersonic Winged Rocket (page 29). Fold the near flap over the centerline.

2

Valley-fold the top edge of the near flap down to the internal folded edge.

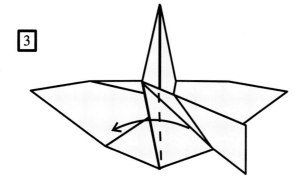

3

Valley-fold the near flap back
along the centerline.

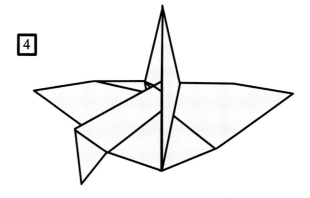

4

Repeat steps 1–3 on the three
remaining flaps.

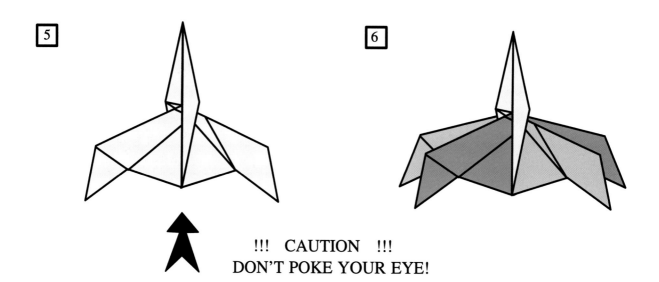

5

6

!!!   CAUTION   !!!
DON'T POKE YOUR EYE!

Grasp opposite fins and inflate
the rocket by blowing
into the hole in the bottom.

Landers

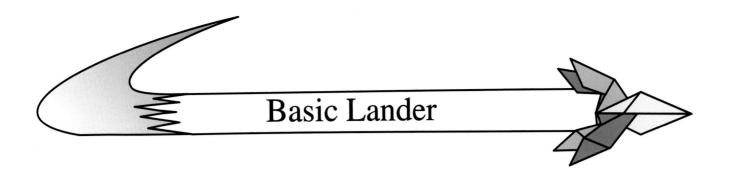

Basic Lander

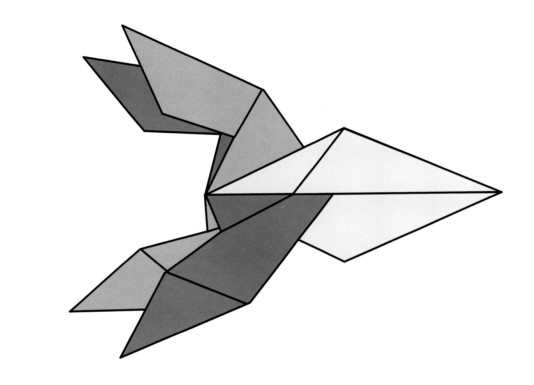

1

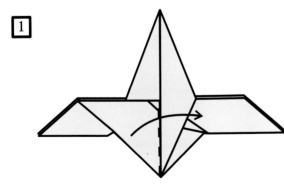

Begin with an uninflated Basic Sweptwing Rocket (page 33).
Swing the near flap all the way over to the right.

2

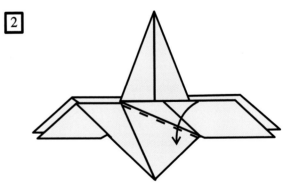

Valley-fold the near flap
down as shown.

3

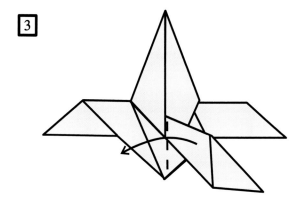

Valley-fold the near flap back
along the centerline.

4

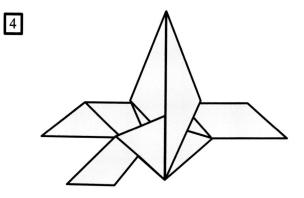

Repeat steps 1–3 on the three remaining flaps.

5

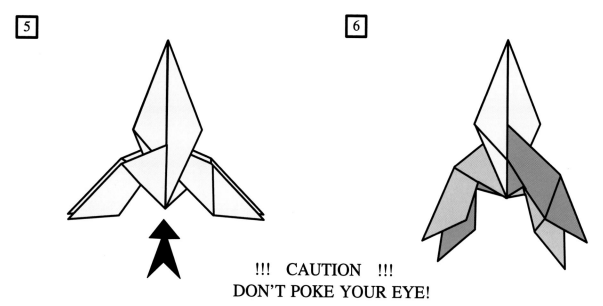

!!! CAUTION !!!
DON'T POKE YOUR EYE!

Grasp opposite fins and inflate
the rocket by blowing into the
hole in the bottom.

6

 **Shortnosed Lander**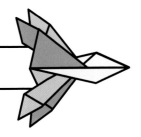

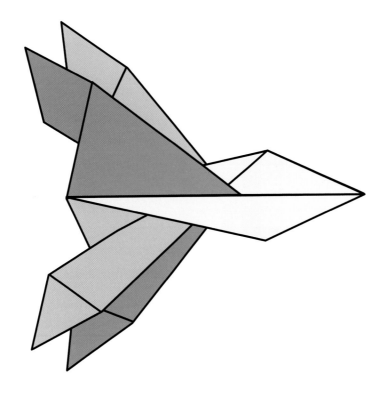

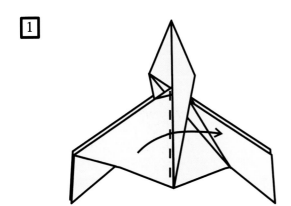

1

Begin with an uninflated Shortnosed Sweptwing Rocket (page 35).
Swing the near wing all the way over to the right.

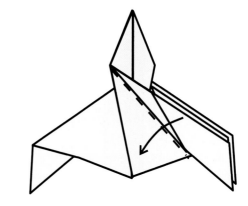

2

Valley-fold the near flap
down as shown.

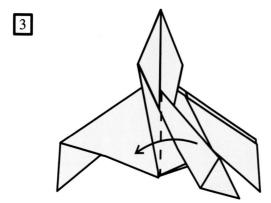

3

Valley-fold the near flap back along the centerline.

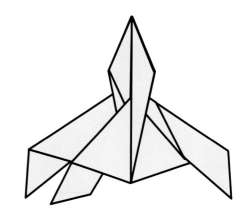

4

Repeat steps 1–3 on the three remaining flaps.

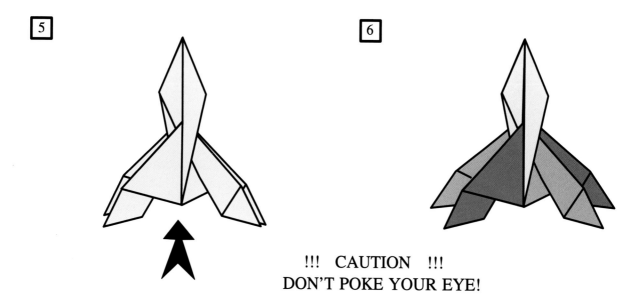

5

Grasp opposite fins and inflate the rocket by blowing into the hole in the bottom.

6

!!! CAUTION !!!
DON'T POKE YOUR EYE!

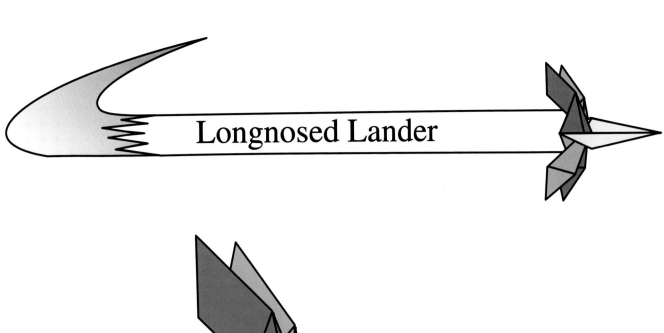

Longnosed Lander

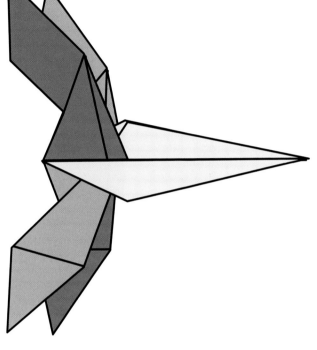

1

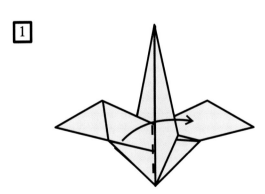

Begin with an uninflated Longnosed Sweptwing Rocket (page 37).
Swing the near left flap all the way over to the right.

2

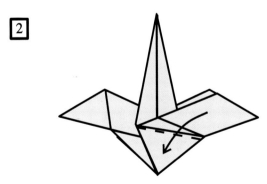

Valley-fold the near flap
down along its own internal
folded edge.

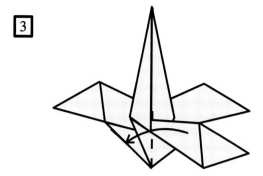

3

Valley-fold the near flap back
along the centerline.

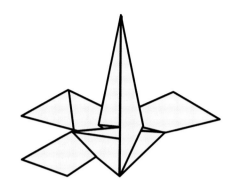

4

Repeat steps 1–3 on the three remaining flaps.

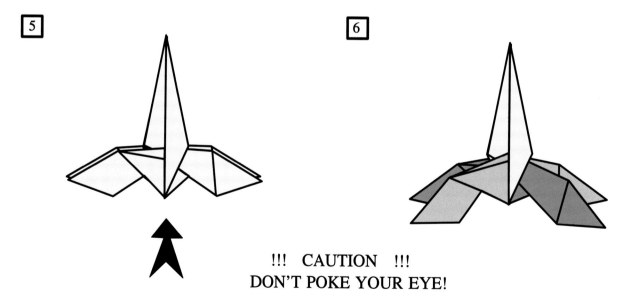

5

Grasp opposite fins and inflate the rocket
by blowing into the hole in the bottom.

6

!!!   CAUTION   !!!
DON'T POKE YOUR EYE!

Supersonic Lander

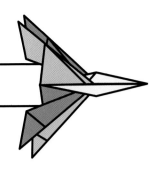

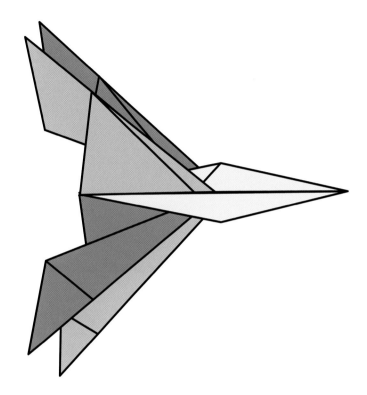

1

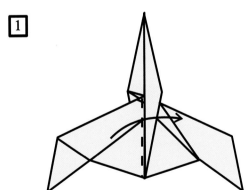

Begin with an uninflated Supersonic Sweptwing Rocket (page 39). Swing the near flap all the way over to the right.

2

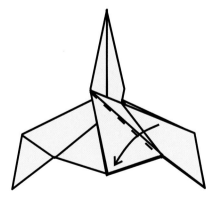

Valley-fold the near flap down as shown.

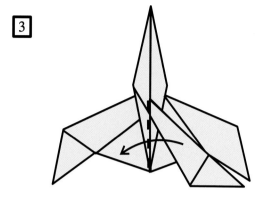

3

Valley-fold the near flap back
along the centerline.

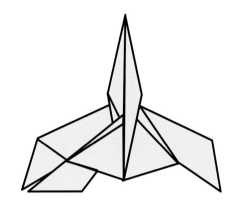

4

Repeat steps 1–3 on the three
remaining flaps of the rocket.

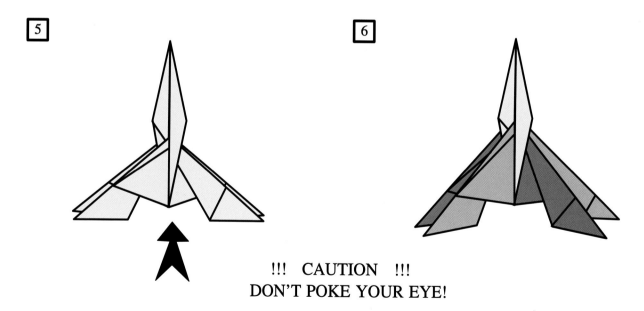

5

Grasp opposite fins and inflate the rocket
by blowing into the hole in the bottom.

6

!!! CAUTION !!!
DON'T POKE YOUR EYE!

Zoomers

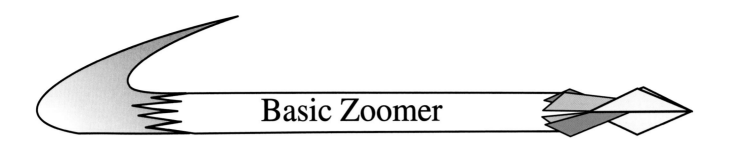

Basic Zoomer

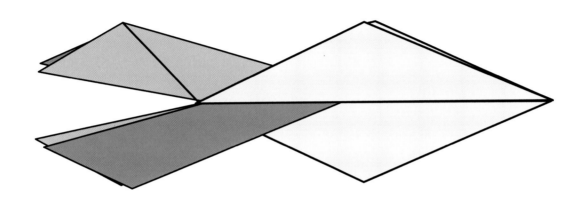

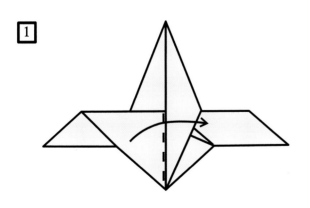

1

Begin with an uninflated Basic Sweptwing Rocket (page 33). Swing the near flap all the way over to the right.

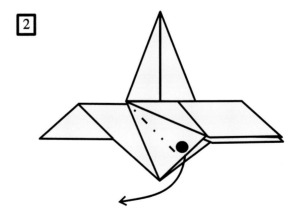

2

Treating two single-layer raw edges as one, pull on the lower right near edge and swivel it clockwise, flattening the entire flap into the position shown in step 3. Watch the black dot.

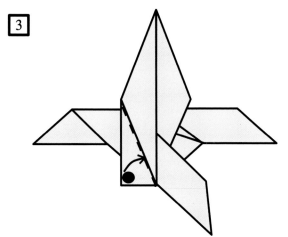

3

Valley-fold the small triangular area, tucking it under the fin as indicated.

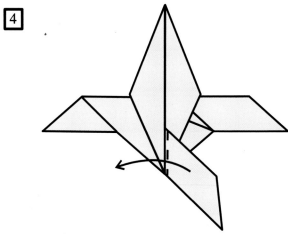

4

Valley-fold the fin leftward over the centerline. Repeat steps 1–4 on the three remaining flaps.

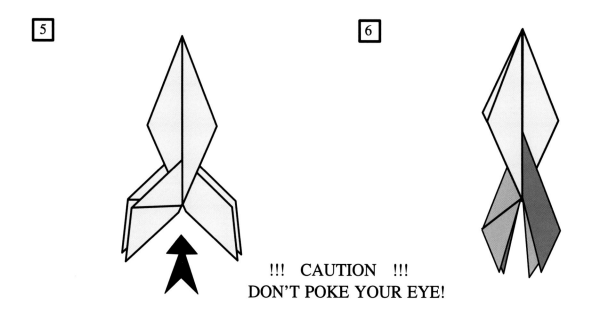

5

6

!!!   CAUTION   !!!
DON'T POKE YOUR EYE!

Grasp opposite fins and inflate the rocket by blowing into the hole in the bottom.

Shortnosed Zoomer

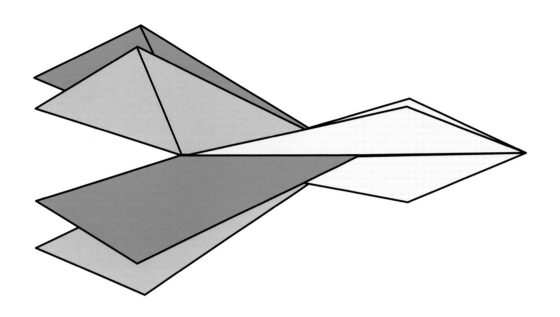

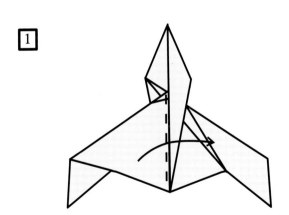

Begin with an uninflated Shortnosed Sweptwing Rocket (page 35). Swing the near left flap all the way over to the right.

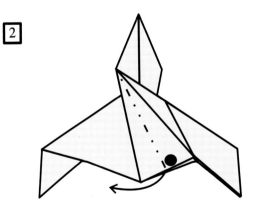

2

Treating two single-layer raw edges as one, pull on the lower right near edge and swivel it clockwise, flattening the entire flap into the position shown in step 3. Watch the black dot.

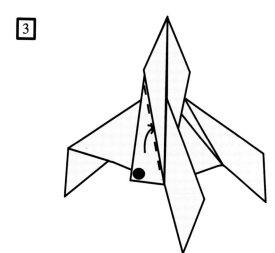

3

Valley-fold the small triangular area, tucking it under the fin as indicated.

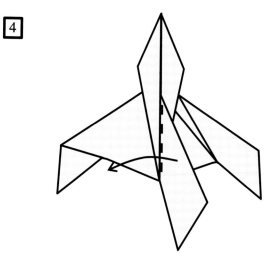

4

Valley-fold the fin leftward over the centerline. Repeat steps 1–4 on the three remaining flaps.

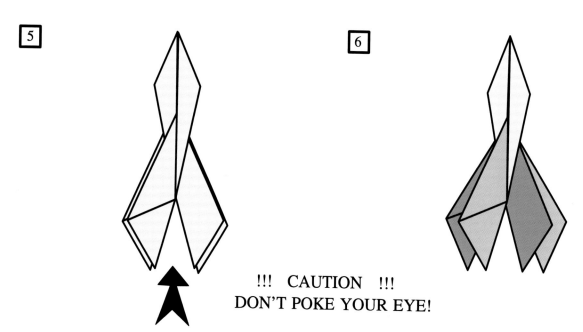

5

6

!!! CAUTION !!!
DON'T POKE YOUR EYE!

Grasp opposite fins and inflate the rocket by blowing into the hole in the bottom.

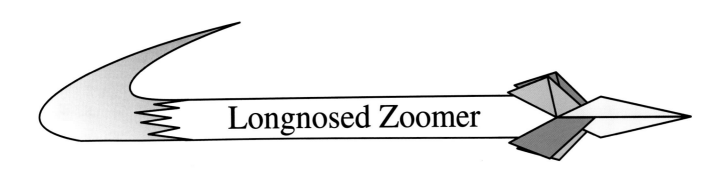

Longnosed Zoomer

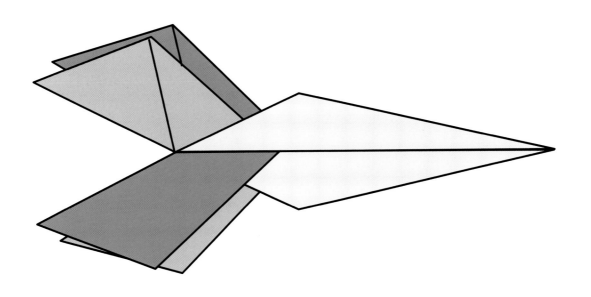

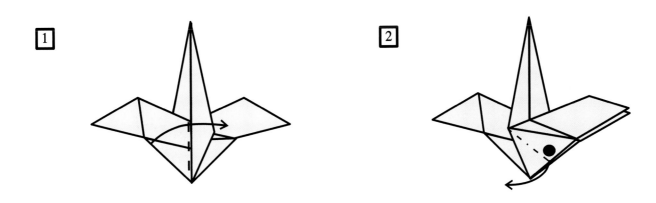

1

Begin with an uninflated Longnosed Sweptwing Rocket (page 37). Swing the near flap all the way over to the right.

2

Treating two single-layer raw edges as one, pull on the lower right near edge and swivel it clockwise, flattening the entire flap into the position shown in step 3. Watch the black dot.

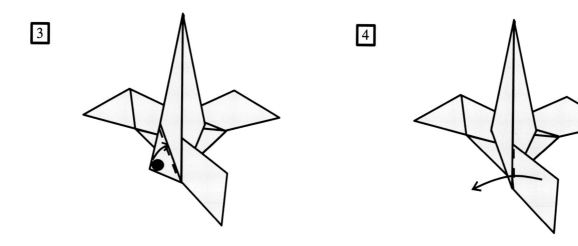

| 3 | | 4 |

Valley-fold the small triangular area, tucking it under the fin as indicated.

Valley-fold the fin leftward over the centerline. Repeat steps 1–4 on the three remaining flaps.

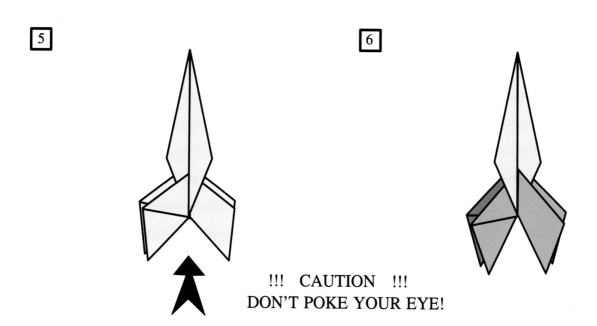

| 5 | | 6 |

!!! CAUTION !!!
DON'T POKE YOUR EYE!

Grasp opposite fins and inflate the rocket by blowing into the hole in the bottom.

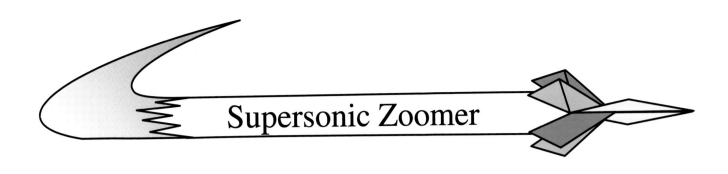

Supersonic Zoomer

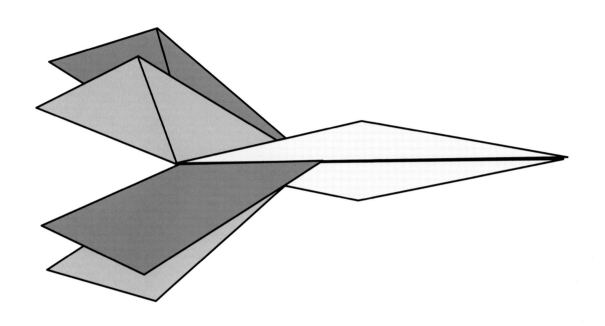

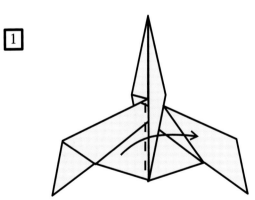

Begin with an uninflated Supersonic Sweptwing Rocket (page 39). Swing the near left flap all the way over to the right.

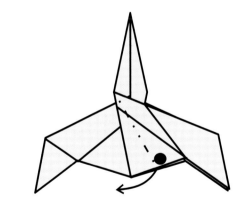

2

Treating two single-layer raw edges as one, pull on the lower right near edge and swivel it clockwise, flattening the entire flap into the position shown in step 3. The crease already exists. Watch the black dot.

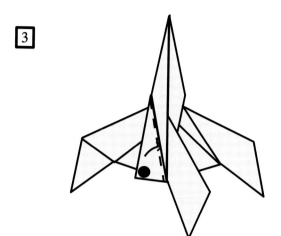

Valley-fold the small triangular area,
tucking it under the fin as indicated.

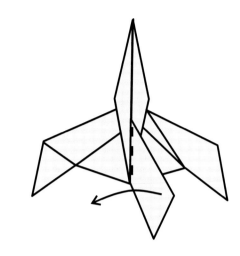

Valley-fold the fin leftward over the centerline.
Repeat steps 1–4 on the three remaining flaps.

5

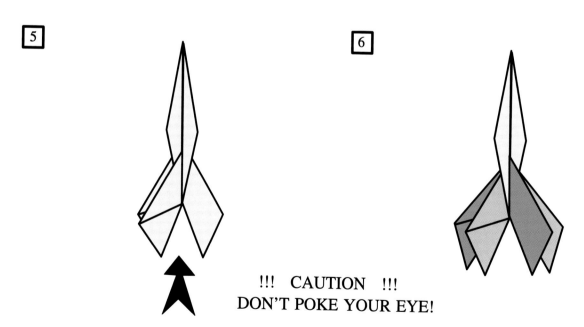

!!! CAUTION !!!
DON'T POKE YOUR EYE!

Grasp opposite fins and inflate the rocket
by blowing into the hole in the bottom.

6

Floaters

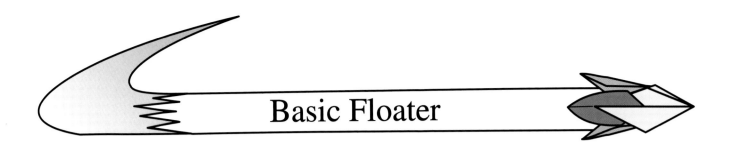

Basic Floater

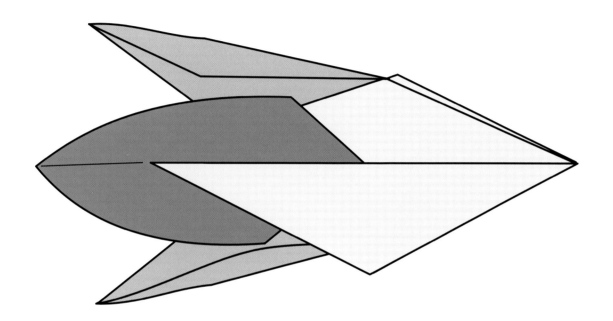

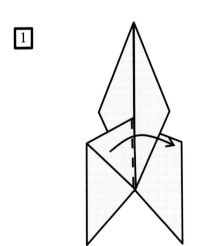

1

Begin with an uninflated Basic Rocket (page 9). Return the near left flap back over the centerline.

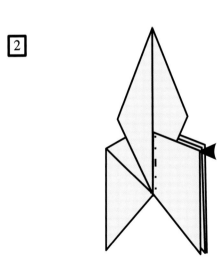

2

Reverse-fold the near right flap leftward along the centerline. It will emerge from the left side.

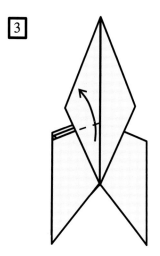

3

Lift and flatten the near flap.

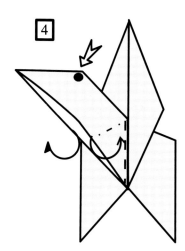

4

Separate the lower edges of the near flap. Press down on the black dot as you pull the raw edges upward–the near layer to the right in front, the far layer toward the left in back. See step 5.

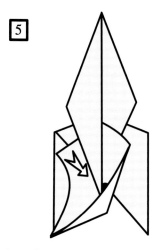

5

The action of step 4 is shown here in progress. The flap must change from convex to concave. Be careful not to tear the paper.

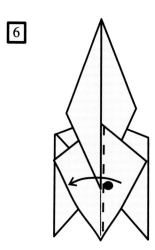

6

The flap as a whole is now concave, like a boat or a cup. Close the flap toward the left. Repeat steps 1–6 on the three remaining flaps.

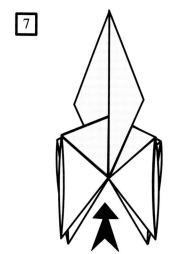

7

Grasp opposite fins and inflate the rocket by blowing into the hole in the bottom.

!!! CAUTION !!!
DON'T POKE YOUR EYE!

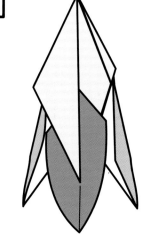

8

Open out the fins to complete the Basic Floater.

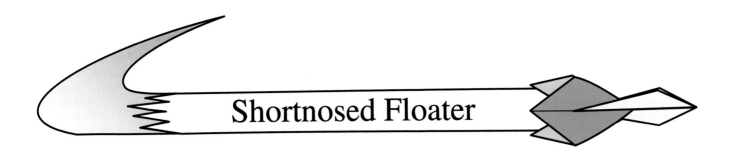

Shortnosed Floater

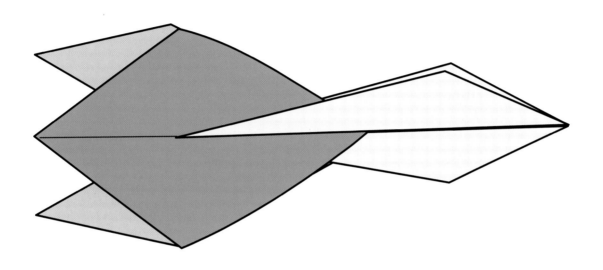

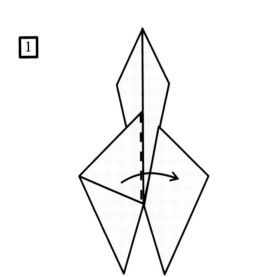

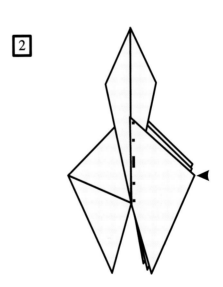

Begin with an uninflated Shortnosed Rocket (page 11). Return the near left flap back over the centerline.

Reverse-fold the near right flap leftward along the centerline. It will emerge from the left side.

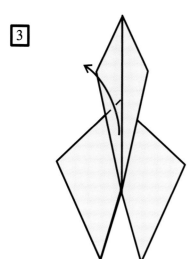

3

Lift the near flap upward as
far as it will go and flatten
the model.

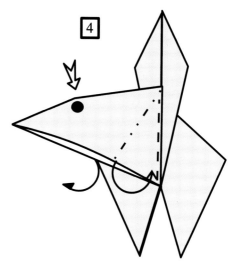

4

Separate the lower edges of the near flap. Press down on the
black dot as you pull the raw edges upward–the near layer to
the right in front, the far layer toward the left in back. See
step 5.

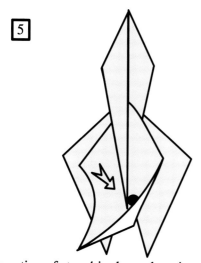

5

The action of step 4 is shown here in progress.
The flap must changefrom convex to concave.
Be careful not to tear the paper.

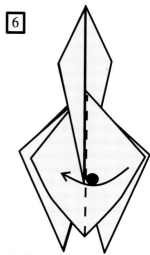

6

The flap as a whole is now concave, like a boat or cup.
Close the flap toward the left. Repeat steps 1–6
on the three remaining flaps.

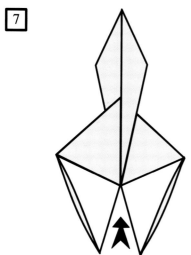

7

Grasp opposite fins and inflate the rocket
by blowing into the hole in the bottom.

!!! CAUTION !!!
DON'T POKE YOUR EYE!

8

Open out the fins to complete the
Shortnosed Floater.

Longnosed Floater

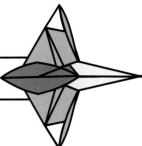

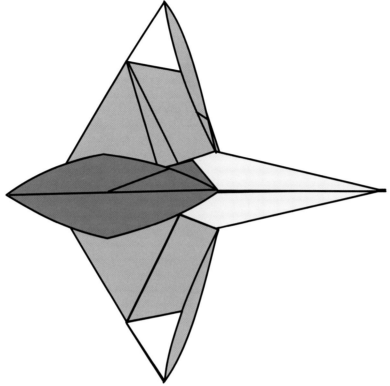

 1

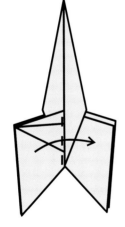

Begin with an uninflated
Longnosed Rocket (page 13).
Return the near left flap
back over the centerline.

2

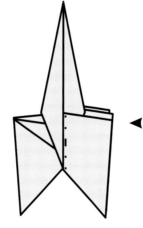

Reverse-fold the right flap
leftward along the centerline.
It will emerge from the left side.

3

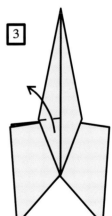

Lift the near flap upward
as far as it will go.

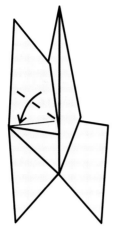

4

Valley-fold the near flap downward so that its right edge touches the lower left corner as shown in step 5.

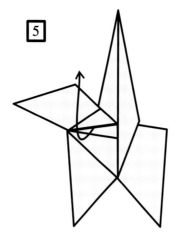

5

Unfold the near flap. returning it to its former position.

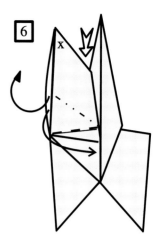

6

Separate the left edges of the near flap. Press down gently on the top right corner as you pull the center of the near raw edge toward the front, and the center of the far raw edge toward the back. Watch the spot marked x. The flap will become a dome.

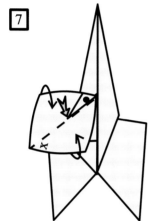

7

Press toward the back on the peak of the dome, as indicated by the hollow arrow; at the same time pull the upper and lower corners of the dome toward the front. The convex dome must become a concave bowl. Watch the black dot, and be careful not to tear the paper.

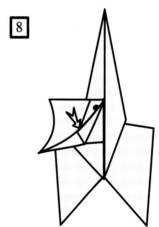

8

The action of step 7 is shown here in progress. Continue to close the flap upward.

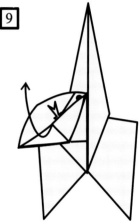

9

The flap as a whole is now concave, like a boat or cup. Close the flap toward the left. Repeat steps 1–9 on the three remaining flaps.

**!!! CAUTION !!!
DON'T POKE YOUR EYE!**

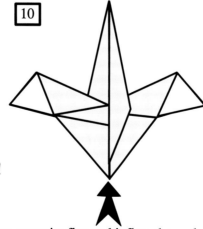

10

Grasp opposite fins and inflate the rocket by blowing into the hole in the bottom.

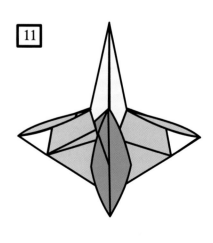

11

Open out the fins to complete the Longnosed Floater.

Supersonic Floater

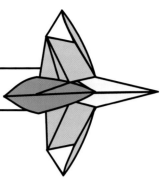

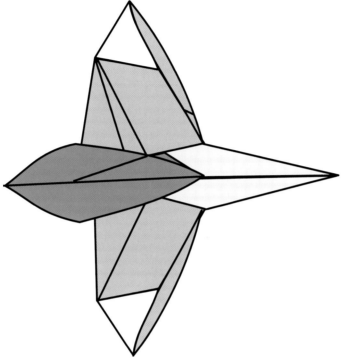

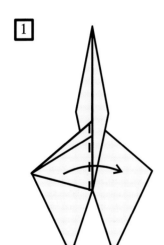

1

Begin with an uninflated Supersonic Rocket (page 17). Return the near left flap back over the centerline.

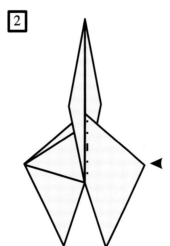

2

Reverse-fold the right flap leftward along the centerline. It will emerge from the left side.

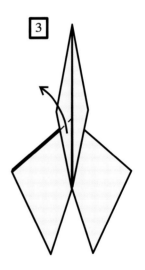

3

Lift the near flap upward as far as it will go.

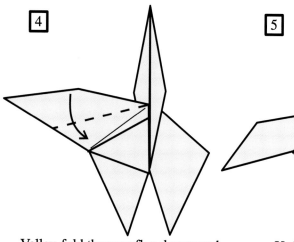

4

Valley-fold the near flap downward so that its right edge touches the lower left corner as shown in step 5.

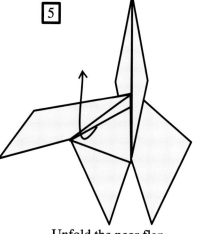

5

Unfold the near flap. returning it to its former position.

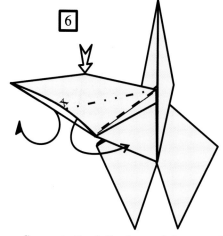

6

Separate the left edges of the near flap. Press down gently on the top right corner as you pull the center of the near raw edge toward the front, and the center of the far raw edge toward the back. Watch the spot marked x. The flap will become a dome.

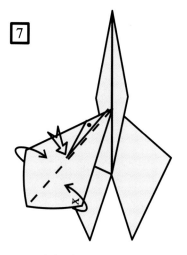

7

Press toward the back on the peak of the dome, as indicated by the hollow arrow; at the same time pull the upper and lower corners of the dome toward the front. The convex dome must become a concave bowl. Watch the black dot, and be careful not to tear the paper.

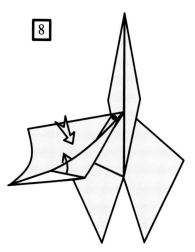

8

The action of step 7 is shown here in progress. Continue to close the flap upward.

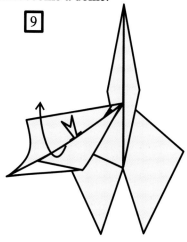

9

The flap as a whole is now concave, like a boat or cup. Close the flap toward the left. Repeat steps 1–9 on the three remaining flaps.

!!! CAUTION !!!
DON'T POKE YOUR EYE!

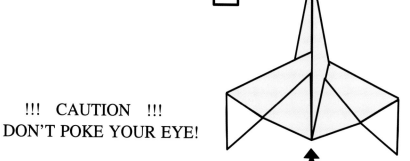

10

Grasp opposite fins and inflate the rocket by blowing into the hole in the bottom.

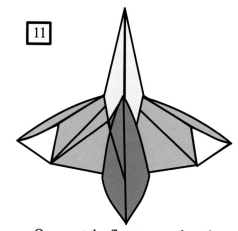

11

Open out the fins to complete the Supersonic Floater.

Gliders

Basic Glider

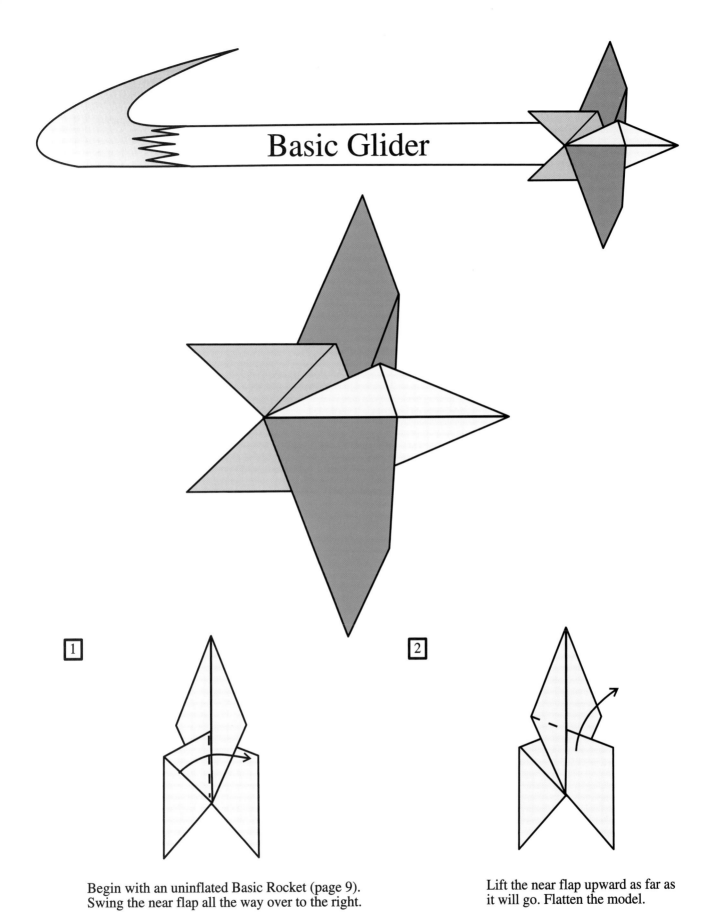

1

Begin with an uninflated Basic Rocket (page 9). Swing the near flap all the way over to the right.

2

Lift the near flap upward as far as it will go. Flatten the model.

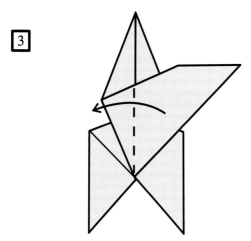

3

Valley-fold the near flap back
to the left along the centerline.

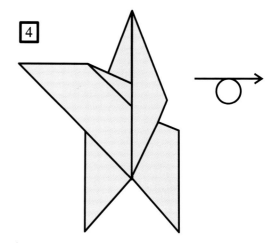

4

Turn the model over and repeat
steps 1–3 behind.

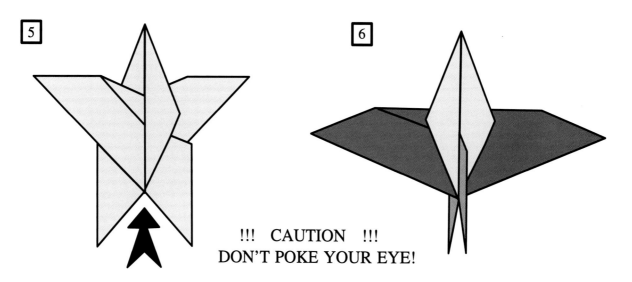

5

!!! CAUTION !!!
DON'T POKE YOUR EYE!

Grasp opposite fins and inflate the rocket
by blowing into the hole in the bottom.

6

Shortnosed Glider

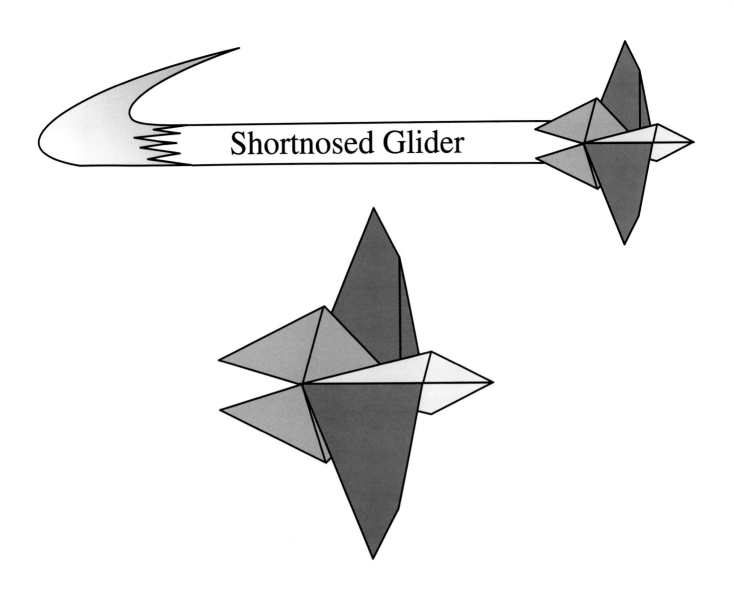

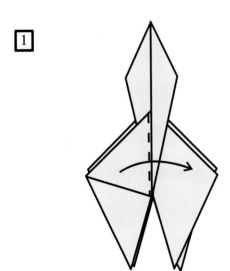

1

Begin with an uninflated Shortnosed Rocket (page 11). Swing the near flap all the way over to the right.

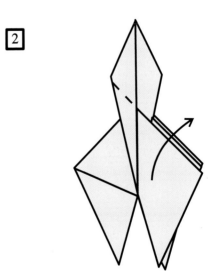

2

Lift the near flap upward as far as it will go. Flatten the model.

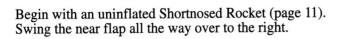

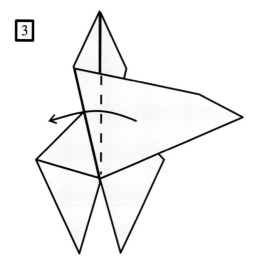

3

Valley-fold the near flap back
to the left along the centerline.

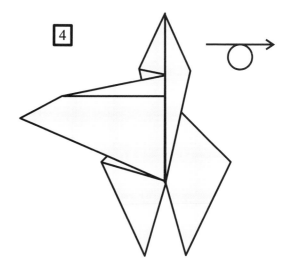

4

Turn the model over and repeat
steps 1–3 behind.

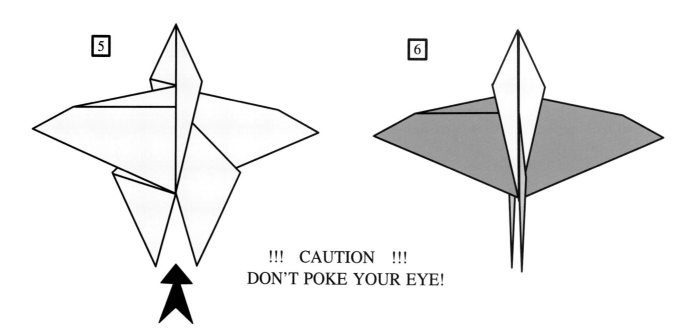

5

Grasp opposite fins and inflate the rocket
by blowing into the hole in the bottom.

6

!!! CAUTION !!!
DON'T POKE YOUR EYE!

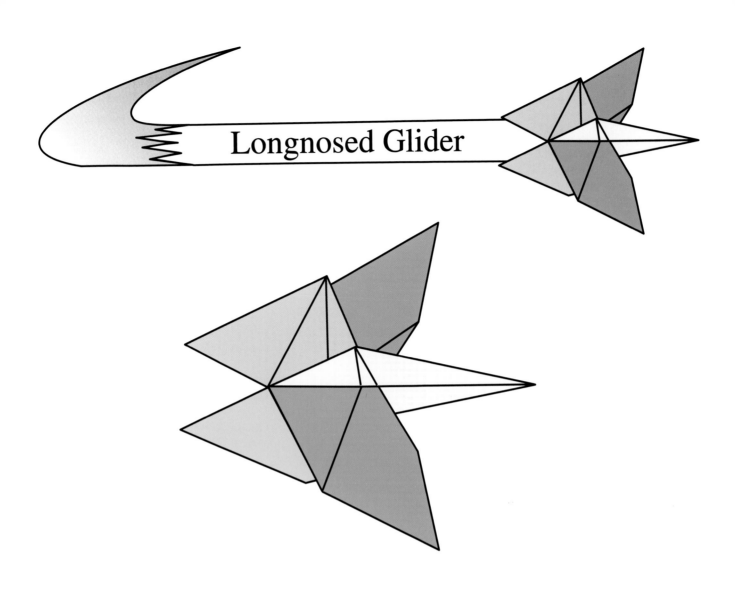

Longnosed Glider

 **1**

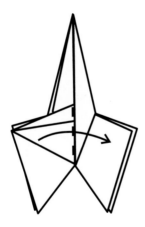

Begin with an uninflated Longnosed Rocket (page 13). Swing the near flap all the way over to the right.

2

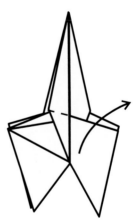

Lift the near flap upward as far as it will go. Flatten the model.

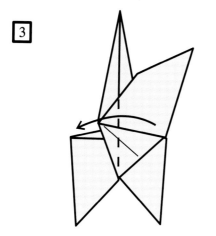

3

Valley-fold the near flap back to
the left along the centerline.

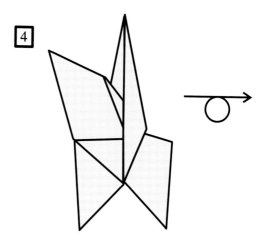

4

Turn the model over and repeat
steps 1–3 behind.

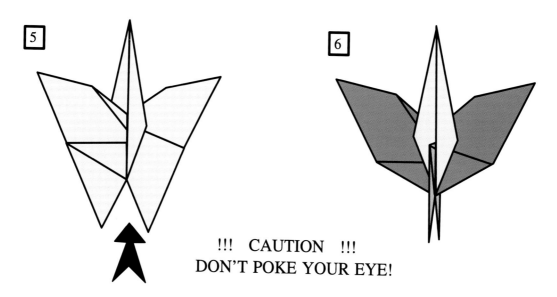

5

Grasp opposite fins and inflate the rocket
by blowing into the hole in the bottom.

!!! CAUTION !!!
DON'T POKE YOUR EYE!

6

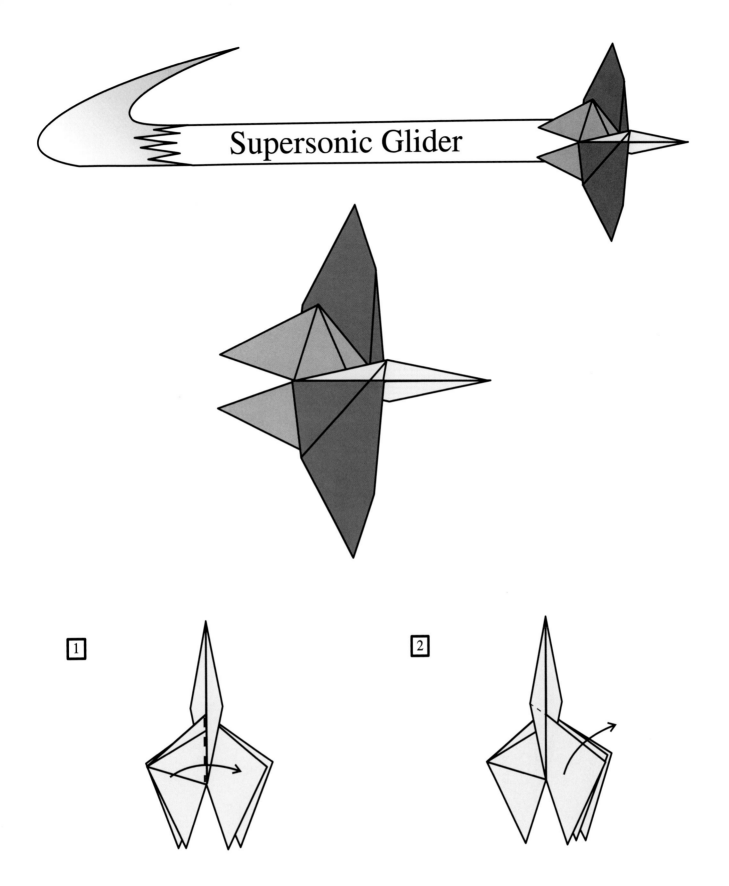

Supersonic Glider

1

Begin with an uninflated Supersonic Rocket (page 17). Swing the near flap all the way over to the right.

2

Lift the near flap upward as far as it will go. Flatten the model.

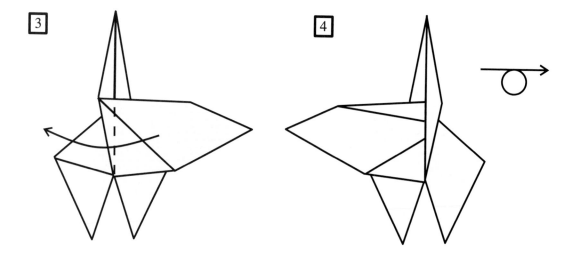

3

Valley-fold the near flap back
to the left along the centerline.

4

Turn the model over and repeat
steps 1–3 behind.

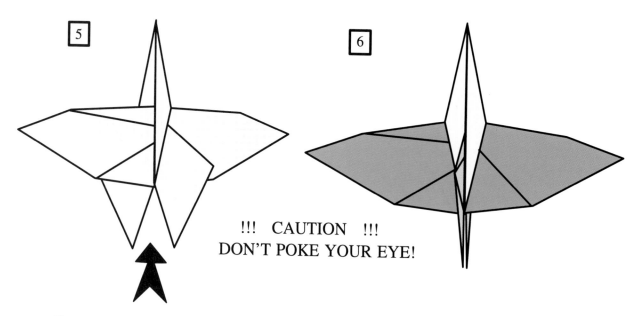

5

!!!   CAUTION   !!!
DON'T POKE YOUR EYE!

6

Grasp opposite fins and inflate the rocket
by blowing into the hole in the bottom.

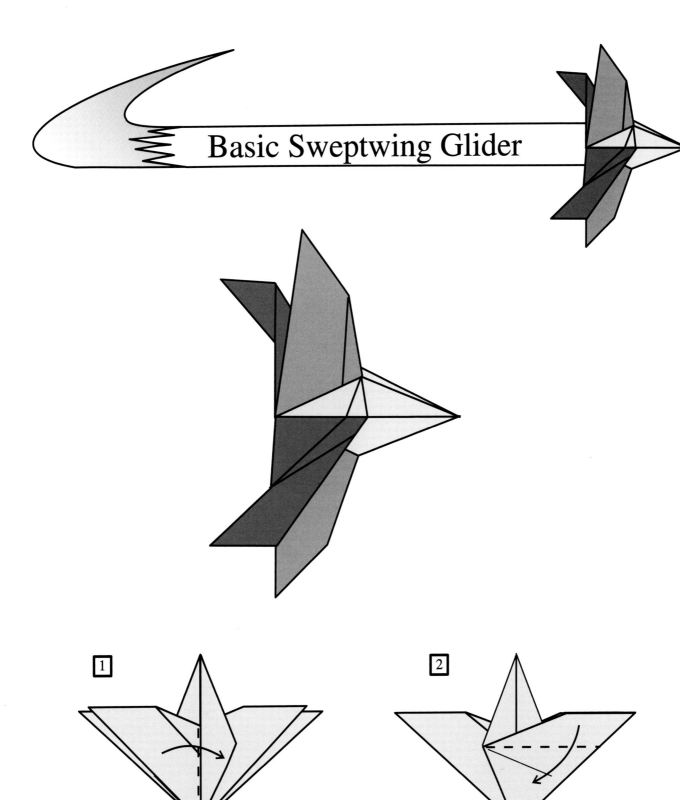

Basic Sweptwing Glider

1

2

Begin with an uninflated Basic Winged Rocket (page 23). Swing the near flap all the way over to the right.

Valley-fold the upper part of the near flap down to form a sweptwing fin. The crease should be horizontal.

3

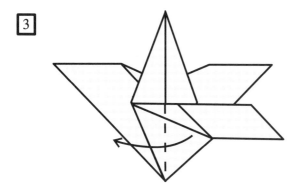

Valley-fold the near flap back
to the left along the centerline.

4

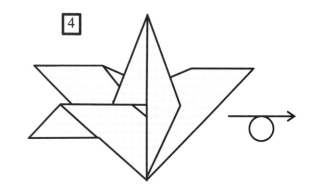

Turn the model over and
repeat steps 1–3 behind.

5

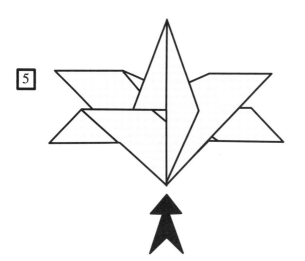

Grasp opposite fins and inflate the rocket
by blowing into the hole in the bottom.

6

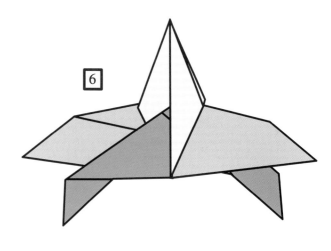

!!!   CAUTION   !!!
DON'T POKE YOUR EYE!

Shortnosed Sweptwing Glider

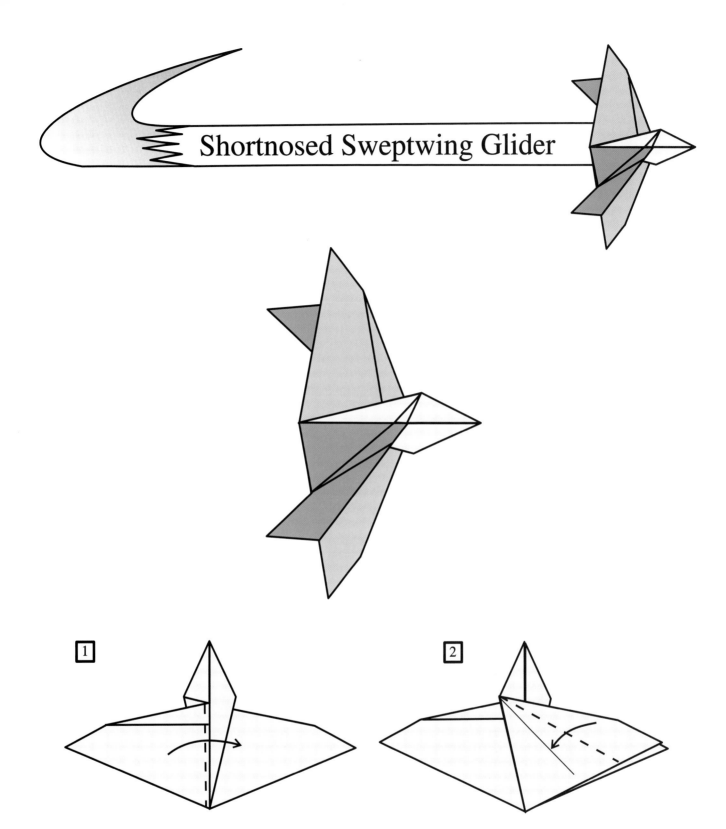

1

Begin with an uninflated Shortnosed Winged Rocket (page 25). Swing the near flap all the way to the right.

2

Valley-fold the upper part of the near flap down to the existing crease to form a sweptwing fin.

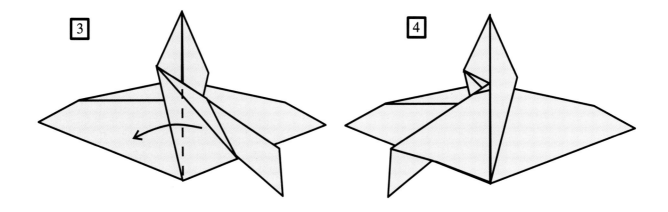

Valley-fold the near flap back
to the left along the centerline.

Turn the model over and repeat
steps 1 – 3 behind.

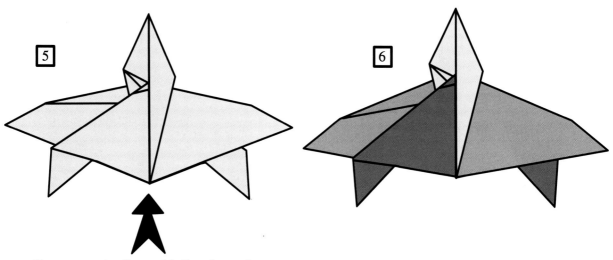

5

6

Grasp opposite fins and inflate the rocket
by blowing into the hole in the bottom.

!!! CAUTION !!!
DON'T POKE YOUR EYE!

 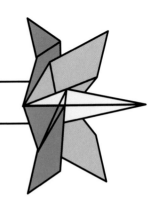

Longnosed Sweptwing Glider

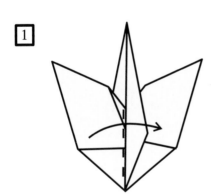

1

Begin with an uninflated Longnosed Winged Rocket (page 27). Swing the near flap all the way over to the right. Flatten the model.

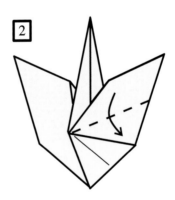

2

Valley-fold the top left edge of the near flap down to the internal folded edge to form a sweptwing fin.

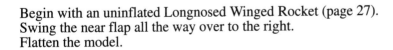

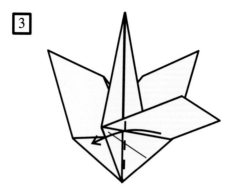

3

Valley fold the near flap back
to the left along the centerline.

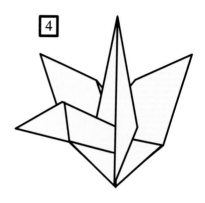

4

Turn the model over and repeat
steps 1–3 behind.

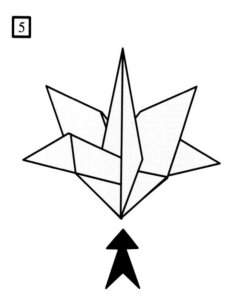

5

Grasp opposite fins and inflate the rocket
by blowing into the hole in the bottom.

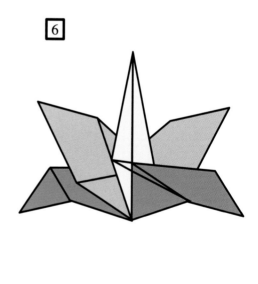

6

!!!   CAUTION   !!!
DON'T POKE YOUR EYE!

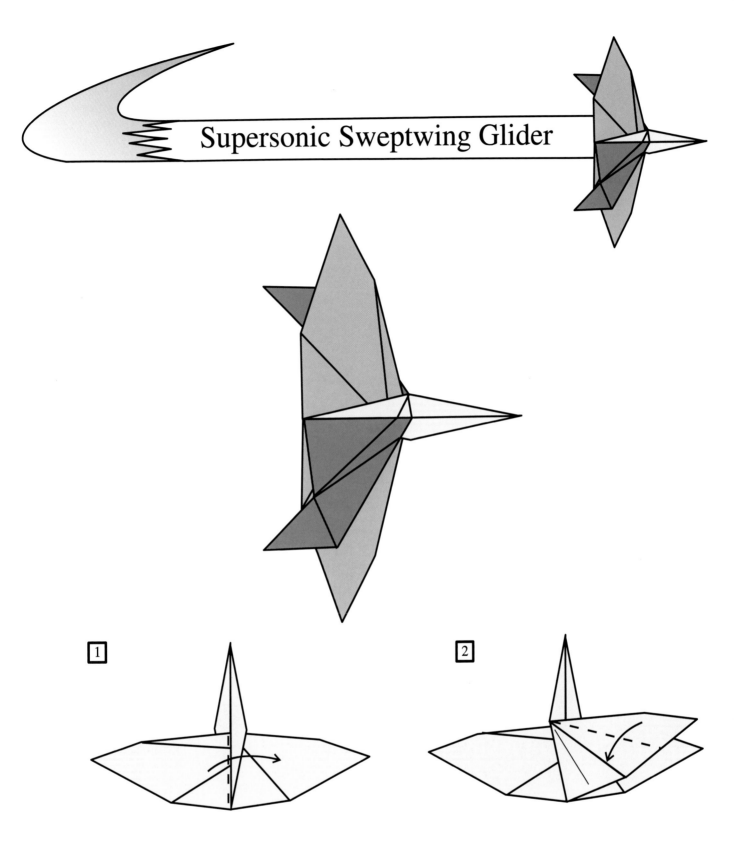

Supersonic Sweptwing Glider

1

Begin with an uninflated Supersonic Winged Rocket (page 29). Swing the near flap all the way over to the right.

2

Valley-fold the upper edge of the near flap down to the internal edge to form a sweptwing fin.

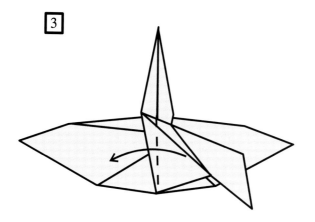

3

Valley-fold the near flap back to the left along the centerline.

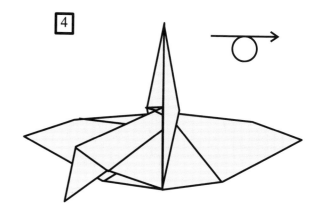

4

Turn the model over and repeat steps 1–3 behind.

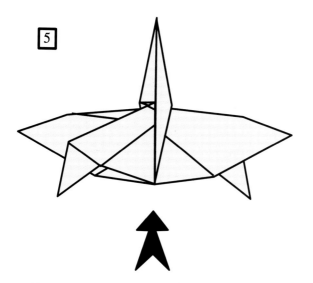

5

Grasp opposite fins and inflate the rocket by blowing into the hole in the bottom.

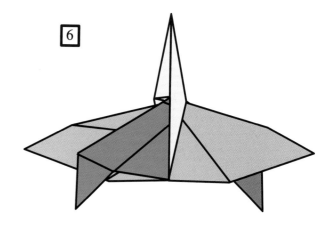

6

!!!   CAUTION   !!!
DON'T POKE YOUR EYE!

Zoomer Gliders

Basic Zoomer Glider

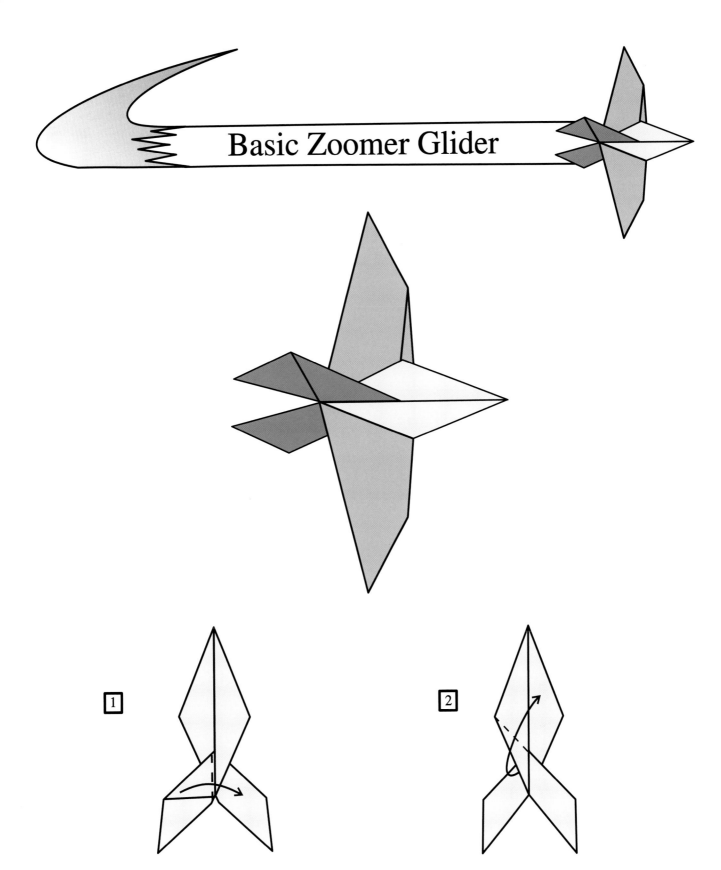

1. Begin with an uninflated Basic Zoomer (page 53).
   Swing the near flap all the way to the right.

2. Open the near flap upward.

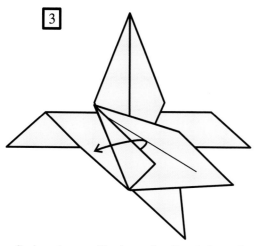

Swing the small triangular flap leftward.

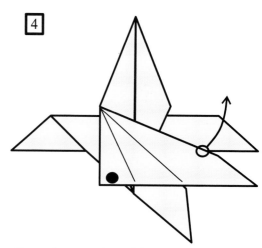

Grasp the top edge of the wing and swivel it upward counterclockwise. Watch the black dot.

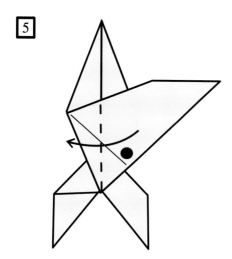

Valley-fold the wing leftward along the centerline.

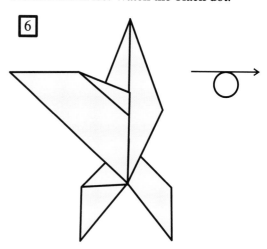

Turn the model over and repeat steps 1–5 behind.

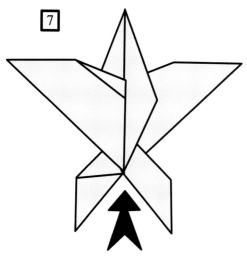

Grasp opposite fins and inflate the rocket by blowing into the hole in the bottom.

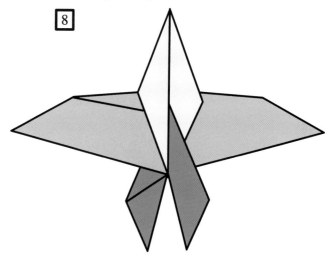

!!! CAUTION !!!
DON'T POKE YOUR EYE!

Shortnosed Zoomer Glider

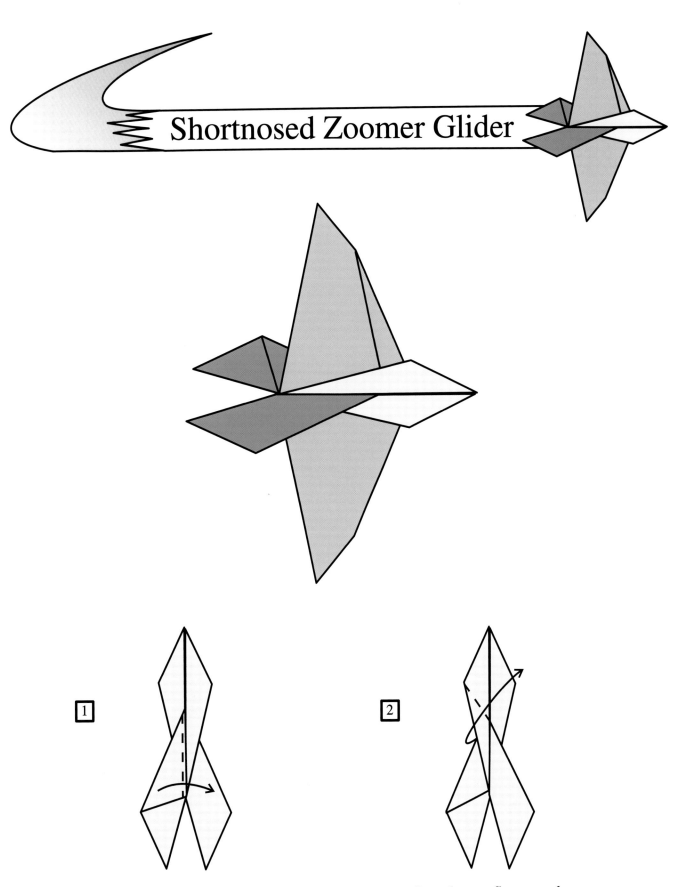

1

Begin with an uninflated Shortnosed Zoomer (page 55).
Swing the near flap all the way over to the right.

2

Open the near flap upward.

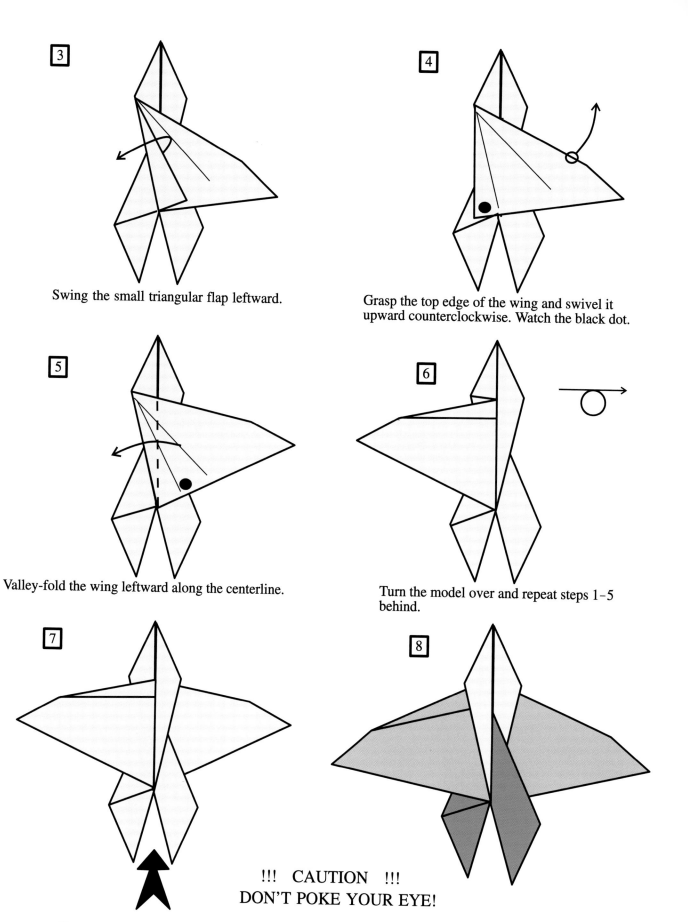

3 Swing the small triangular flap leftward.

4 Grasp the top edge of the wing and swivel it upward counterclockwise. Watch the black dot.

5 Valley-fold the wing leftward along the centerline.

6 Turn the model over and repeat steps 1–5 behind.

7 Grasp opposite fins and inflate the rocket by blowing into the hole in the bottom.

!!! CAUTION !!!
DON'T POKE YOUR EYE!

8

Longnosed Zoomer Glider

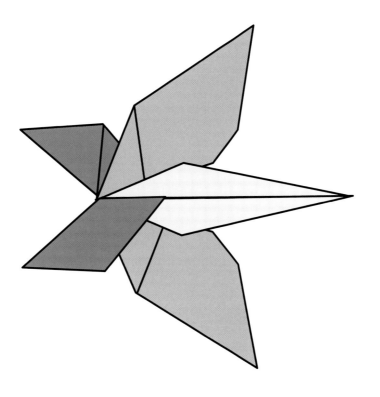

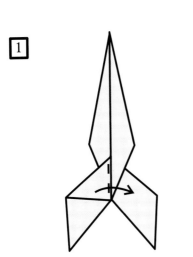

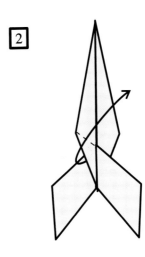

Begin with an uninflated Longnosed Zoomer (page 57). Swing the near flap all the way over to the right.

Open the near flap upward.

3

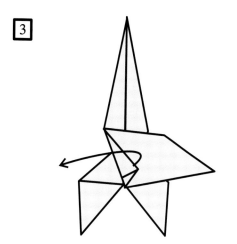

Swing the small triangular flap leftward.

4

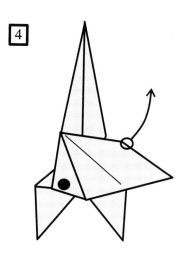

Grasp the top edge of the wing and swivel it upward counterclockwise. Watch the black dot.

5

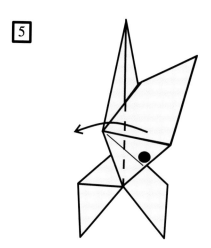

Valley-fold the near flap leftward along the centerline.

6

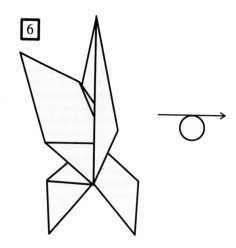

Turn the model over and repeat steps 1–5 behind.

7

!!! CAUTION !!!
DON'T POKE YOUR EYE!

Grasp opposite fins and inflate the rocket
by blowing into the hole in the bottom.

8

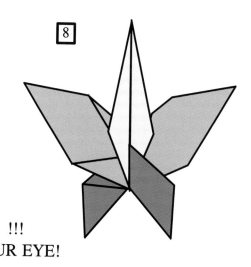

Supersonic Zoomer Glider

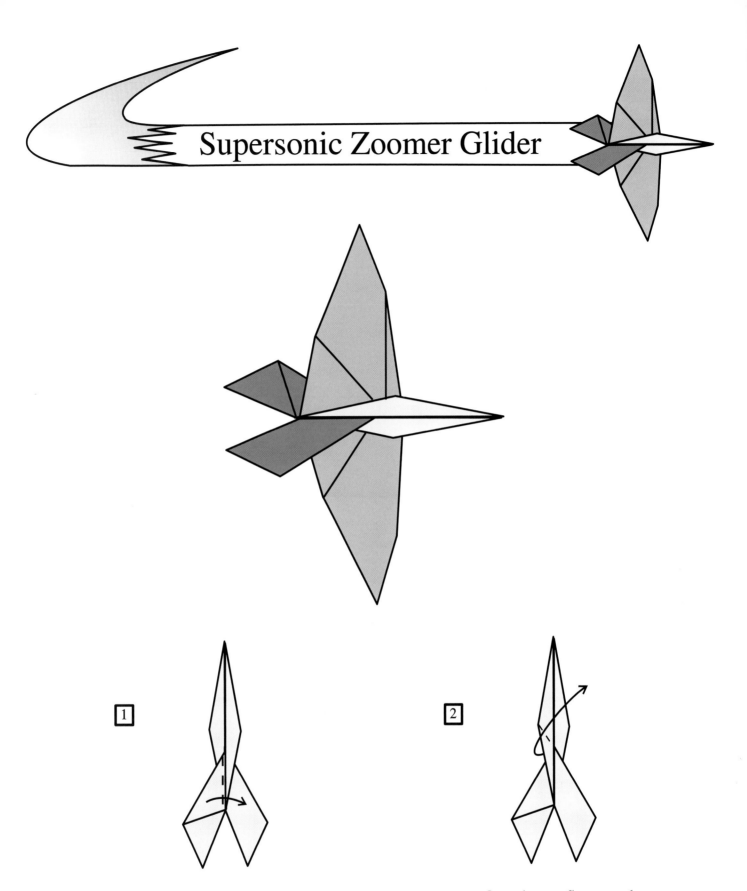

☐1

Begin with an uninflated Supersonic Zoomer (page 59).
Swing the near flap all the way over to the right.

☐2

Open the near flap upward.

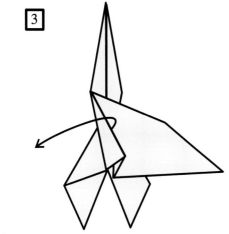

3

Swing the small triangular flap leftward.

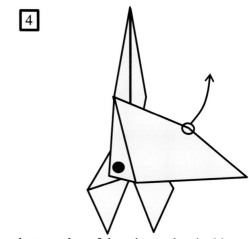

4

Grasp the top edge of the wing and swivel it
upward counterclockwise. Watch the black dot.

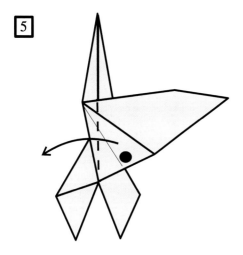

5

Valley-fold the wing leftward along the centerline.

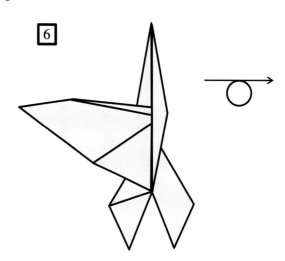

6

Turn the model over and repeat steps 1–5 behind.

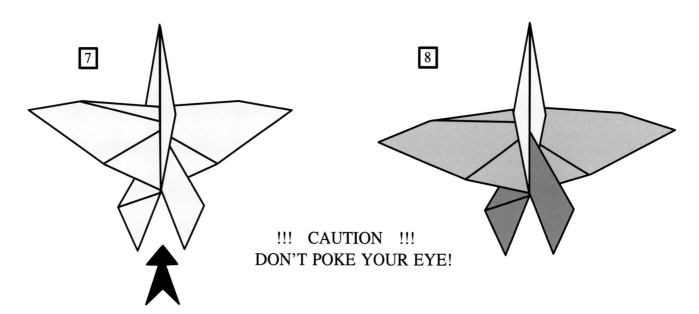

7

Grasp opposite fins and inflate the rocket
by blowing into the hole in the bottom.

!!!   CAUTION   !!!
DON'T POKE YOUR EYE!

8

Soarers

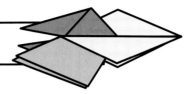

Basic Soarer

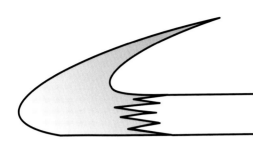

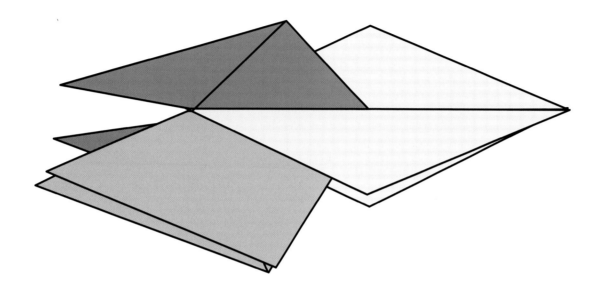

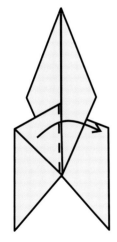

1

Begin with an uninflated Basic
Rocket (page 9).
Return the near left flap back
over the centerline.

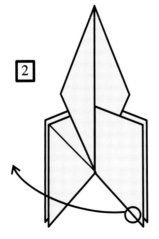

2

Grasp the tip of the near flap
and pull it all the way to the left,
opening the fin completely.

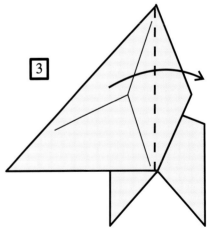

3

Valley-fold the large flap rightward
along the the centerline.

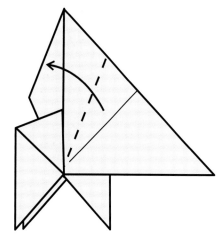

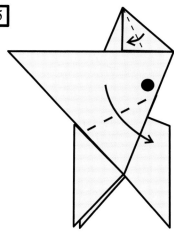

Steps 4–6 show the folding of a fin on the right flap instead of the left. All the folding is done on the existing crease lines. Valley-fold the large flap leftward along an existing crease as shown.

Pull the long edge of the near flap downward; at the same time bring the short top right edge to the vertical centerline. Watch the black dot.

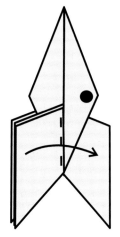
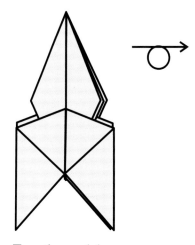

Swing the near flap rightward over the centerline.

Turn the model over.

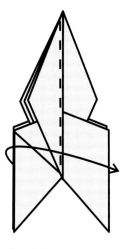
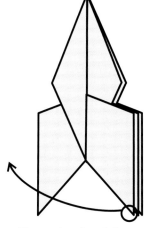

Swing to the right along the centerline both the near left fin and the nearest part of the fuselage.

Grasp the tip of the nearest fin and pull it all the way to the left, opening the flap completely.

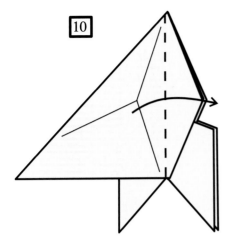

10

Valley-fold the large flap rightward
along the centerline.

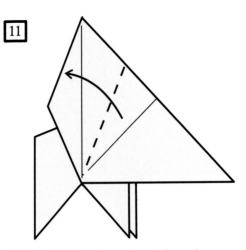

11

Valley-fold the large flap leftward
along an existing crease, as shown.

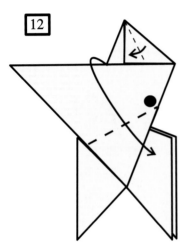

12

Pull the long edge of the near flap downward.
At the same time bring the short top right edge
to the vertical centerline. Watch the black dot.

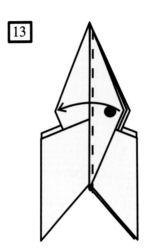

13

Valley-fold to the left the
nearest portion of the fuselage.

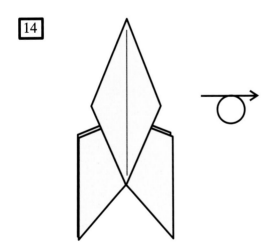

14

Turn the model over.

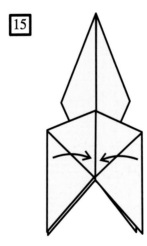

15

Pinch the two near fins together
to form a keel.

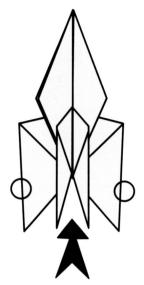

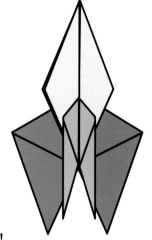

!!!   CAUTION   !!!
DON'T POKE YOUR EYE!

Grasp opposite fins and inflate the rocket by blowing into the hole in the bottom.

In flight the keel will be nearest to the ground— we are looking at the underside of the Soarer.

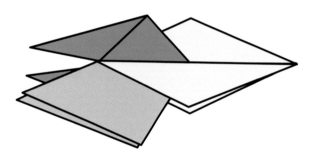

Shortnosed Soarer

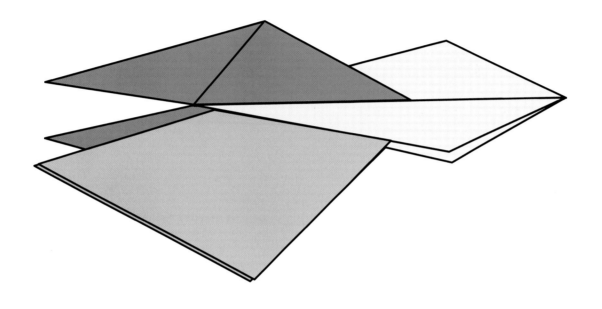

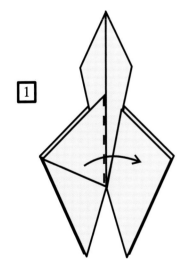

1

Begin with an uninflated
Shortnosed Rocket (page 11).
Return the near left flap back
over the centerline.

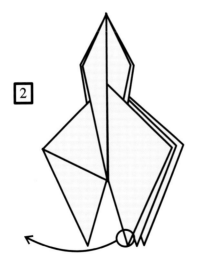

2

Grasp the tip of the near flap and
pull it all the way to the left,
opening the fin completely.

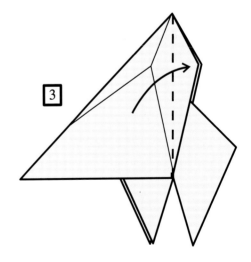

3

Valley-fold the large flap rightward
along the centerline.

4

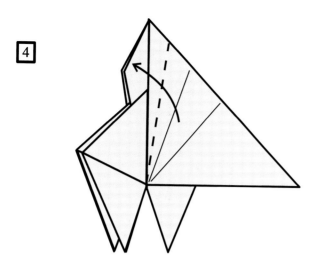

Steps 3–5 show the folding of a fin on the right flap instead of the left. All the folding is done on the existing crease lines. Valley-fold the large flap leftward along an existing crease as shown.

5

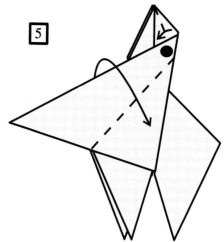

Pull the long edge of the near flap downward; at the same time bring the short top right edge to the vertical centerline. Watch the black dot.

6

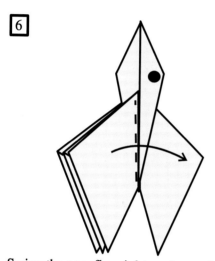

Swing the near flap rightward over the centerline.

7

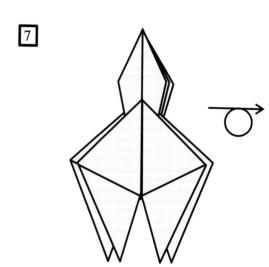

Turn the model over.

8

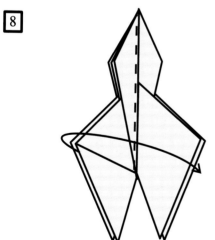

Swing to the right along the centerline both the near left fin and the nearest part of the fuselage.

9

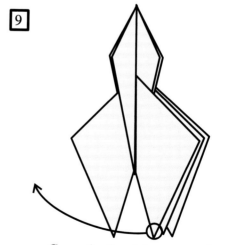

Grasp the tip of the nearest fin and pull it all the way to the left, opening the flap completely.

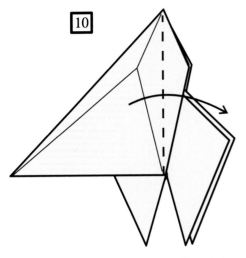

10

Valley-fold the large flap rightward
along the centerline.

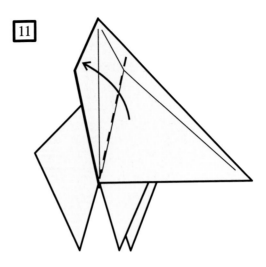

11

Valley-fold the large flap leftward
along an existing crease, as shown.

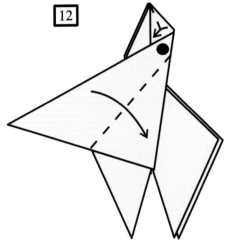

12

Pull the long edge of the near flap downward.
At the same time bring the short top right edge
to the vertical centerline. Watch the black dot.

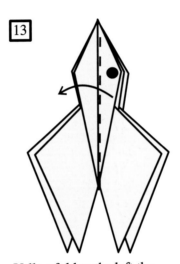

13

Valley-fold to the left the
nearest portion of the fuselage.

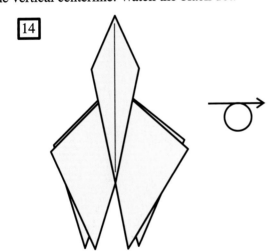

14

Turn the model over.

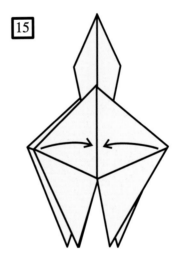

15

Pinch the two near fins together
to form a keel.

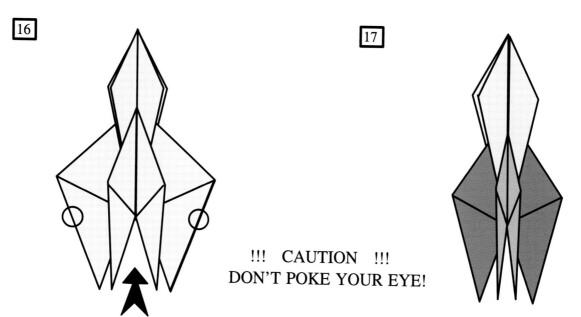

16

Grasp opposite fins and inflate the rocket
by blowing into the hole in the bottom.

!!! CAUTION !!!
DON'T POKE YOUR EYE!

17

In flight the keel will be nearest to the ground–
we are looking at the underside of the soarer

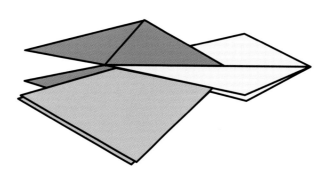

 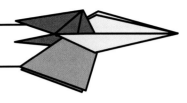

Longnosed Soarer

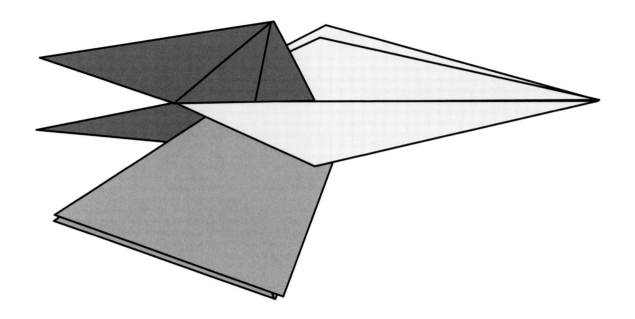

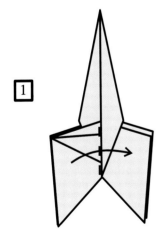

1

Begin with an uniflated
Longnosed Rocket (page 13).
Return the near left flap
back over the centerline.

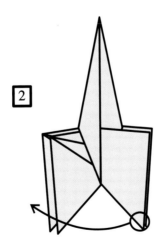

2

Grasp the tip of the near flap and
pull it all the way to the left,
opening the fin completely.

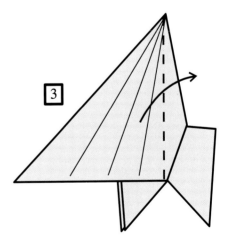

3

Valley-fold the large flap
rightward along the centerline.

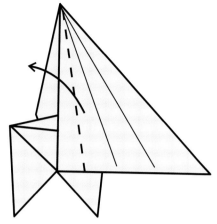

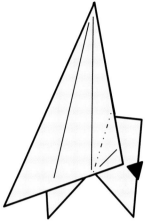

Steps 4–9 show the folding of a fin on the right flap instead of the left. All the folding is done on the existing crease lines. Valley-fold the large flap leftward along an existing crease as shown.

Reverse-fold into the model the lower right corner of the near flap: note carefully the position of the creases.

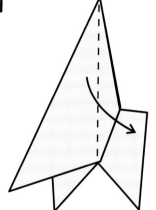

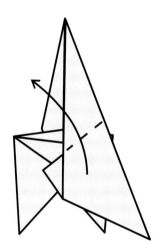

Valley-fold the near flap leftward along the centerline.

Valley-fold the bottom of the near flap upward along part of the existing crease. Don't try to flatten the flap.

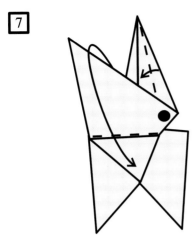

Valley-fold the top part of the nearest flap downward forming a valley crease along the internal folded edge; at the same time bring the far right edge to the centerline. Flatten the model. Watch the black dot.

Swing the near fin all the way over to the right.

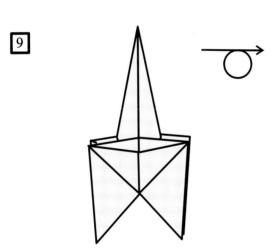

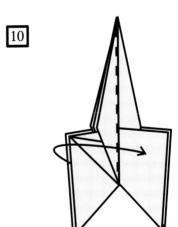

Turn the model over.

Swing to the right along the centerline both the near left fin and the nearest part of the fuselage.

Grasp the tip of the nearest fin
and pull it all the way to the left,
opening the flap completely.

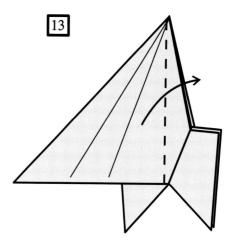

Valley-fold the large flap
rightward along the centerline.

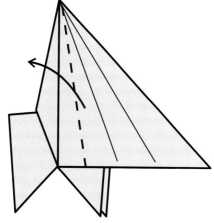

Valley-fold the large flap leftward
along the existing crease as shown.

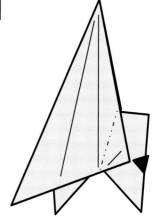

Reverse-fold into the model the lower right
corner of the near flap: note carefully the
position of the existing creases.

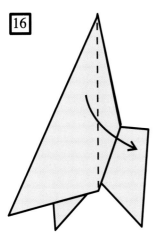

16

Valley-fold the near flap
rightward along the centerline.

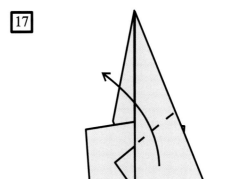

17

Valley-fold the bottom of the near flap
upward along the existing crease.

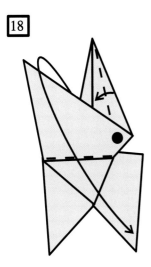

18

Valley-fold the top part of the nearest flap downward,
forming a valley crease along the internal folded edge; at
the same time bring the far right edge to the centerline.
Flatten the model. Watch the black dot.

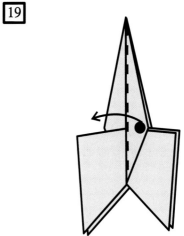

19

Valley-fold to the left the
nearest portion of the fuselage.

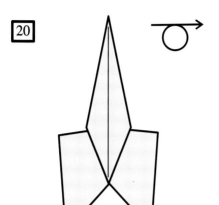 20

Turn the model over.

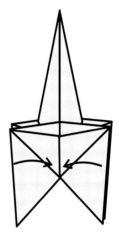 21

Pinch the two near fins together
to form a keel.

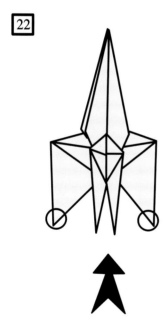 22

Grasp opposite fins and inflate the rocket
by blowing into the hole in the bottom.

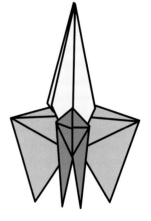 23

In flight the keel will be nearest to the ground—
we are looking at the underside of the soarer.

!!!   CAUTION   !!!
DON'T POKE YOUR EYE!

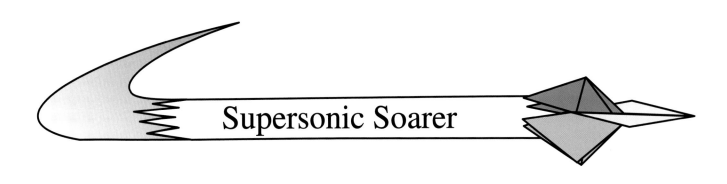

Supersonic Soarer

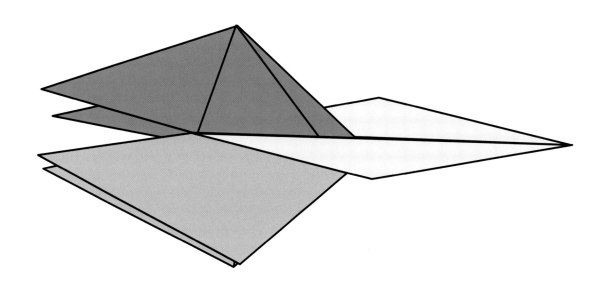

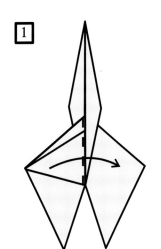

1

Begin with an uniflated
Supersonic Rocket (page 17).
Return the near left flap
back over the centerline.

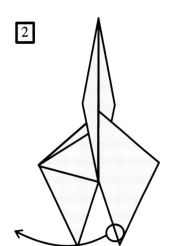

2

Grasp the tip of the near flap and pull
it all the way to the left, opening the
fin completely.

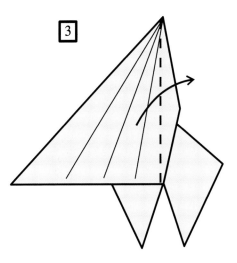

3

Valley-fold the large flap rightward
along the centerline.

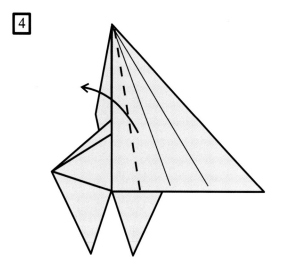

Steps 3–8 show the folding of a fin on the right flap instead of the left. All the folding is done on the existing crease lines. Valley-fold the large flap leftward along an existing crease as shown.

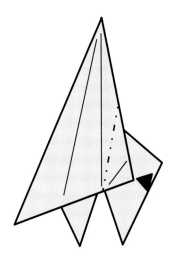

Reverse-fold into the model the lower right corner of the near flap: note carefully the position of the creases.

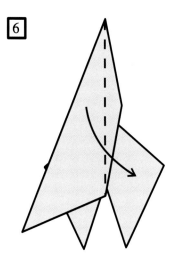

Valley-fold the near flap rightward along the centerline.

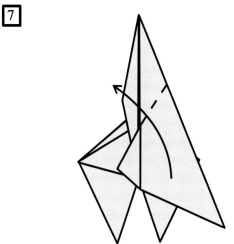

Valley-fold the bottom of the near flap upward along the existing crease.

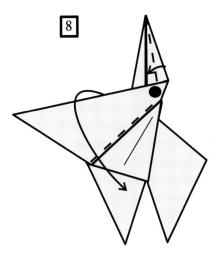

Valley-fold the top part of the nearest flap downward forming a valley crease along the internal folded edge; at the same time bring the far right edge to the centerline. Flatten the model. Watch the black dot.

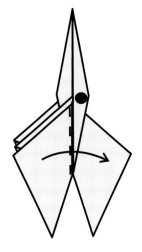

Swing the near fin rightward over the centerline.

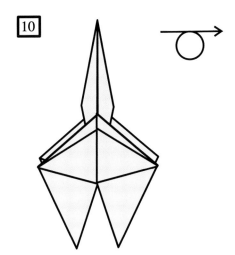

Turn the model over.

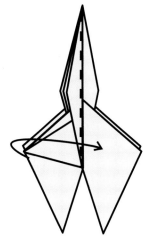

Swing to the right along the centerline both the near left fin and the nearest part of the fuselage.

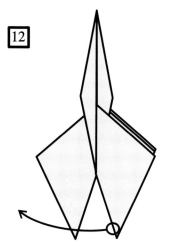

12

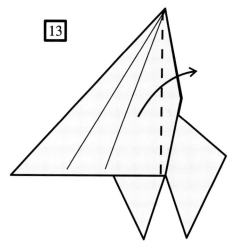

13

Grasp the tip of the nearest fin
and pull it all the way to the left,
opening the flap completely.

Valley-fold the large flap
rightward along the centerline.

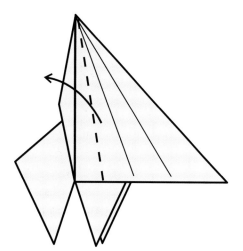

14

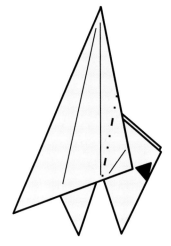

15

Valley-fold the large flap leftward
along the existing crease as shown.

Reverse-fold into the model the lower right
corner of the near flap: note carefully the
position of the existing creases.

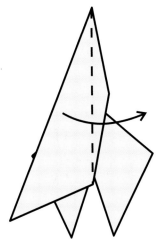

Valley-fold the near flap
rightward along the centerline.

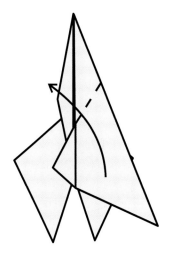

Valley-fold the bottom of the near flap
upward along the existing crease.

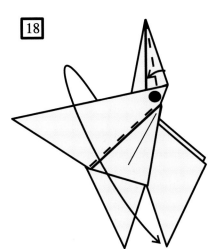

Valley-fold the top part of the nearest flap downward,
forming a valley crease along the internal folded edge; at
the same time bring the far right edge to the centerline.
Flatten the model. Watch the black dot.

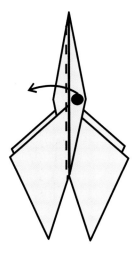

Valley-fold to the left the nearest
portion of the fuselage.

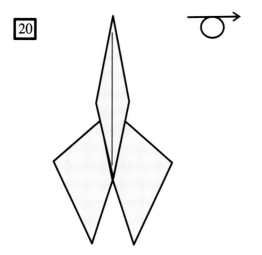

20

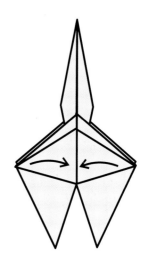

Turn the model over.

21

Pinch the two near fins together
to form a keel.

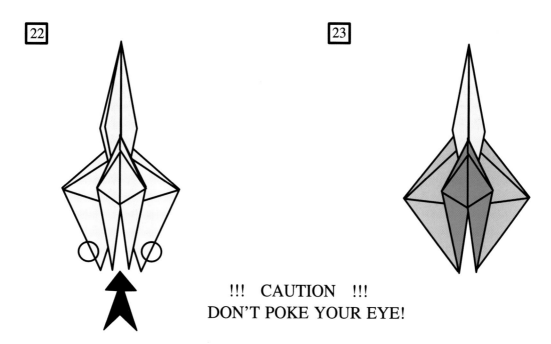

22

Grasp opposite fins and inflate the rocket
by blowing into the hole in the bottom.

23

!!! CAUTION !!!
DON'T POKE YOUR EYE!

In flight the keel will be nearest to the ground—
we are looking at the underside of the soarer.

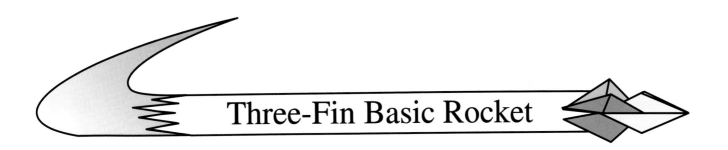

Three-Fin Basic Rocket

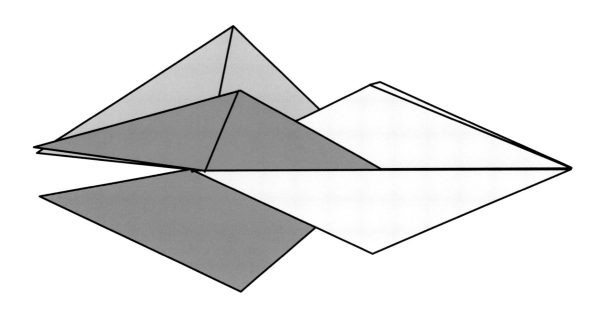

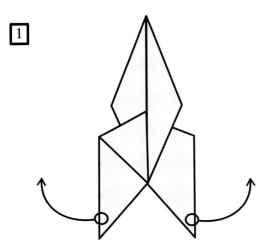

Begin with an uninflated Basic Rocket (page 9). Grasp the tips of the nearest flaps and pull them in opposite directions, opening the fins completely so that they form half of the Waterbomb Base.

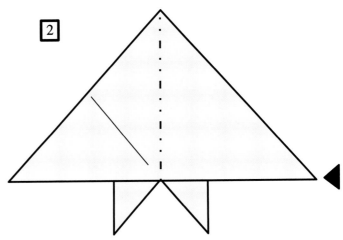

Reverse-fold the near right flap all the way inside the near left flap.

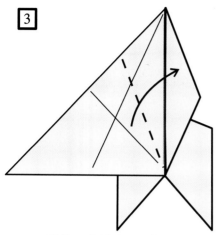

Valley-fold the entire near flap rightward
along an existing crease as shown.

 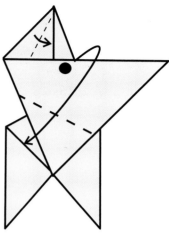

Pull the long upper edge of the near flap downward
along the existing crease as shown. At the same time
bring the short upper left edge to the centerline. Flatten
the model. Watch the black dot.

 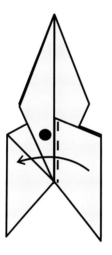

Valley-fold the near fin to the left
along the centerline.

 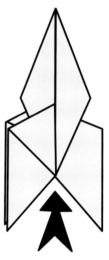

Grasp opposite fins and inflate the rocket
by blowing into the hole in the bottom.

!!! CAUTION !!!
DON'T POKE YOUR EYE!

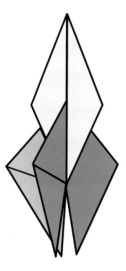

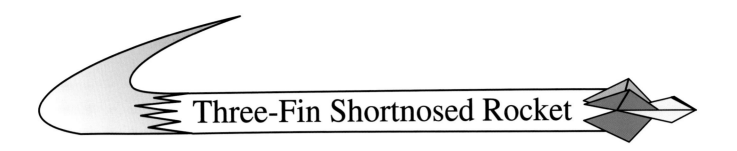

Three-Fin Shortnosed Rocket

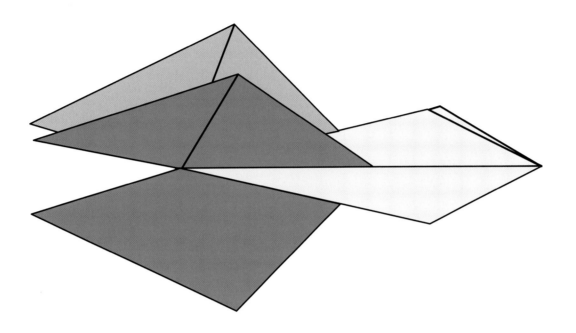

1

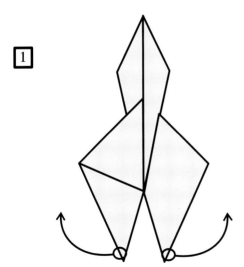

Begin with an uninflated Shortnosed Rocket (page 11).
Grasp the tips of the nearest flaps and pull them in opposite
directions, opening the fins completely so that they form half
of the Waterbomb Base.

2

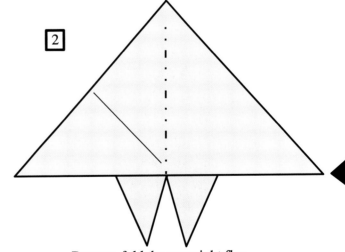

Reverse-fold the near right flap
all the way inside the near left flap.

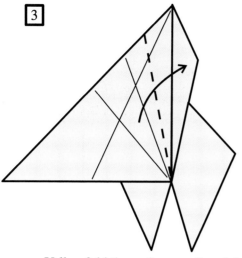

3 Valley-fold the entire near flap rightward along an existing crease as shown.

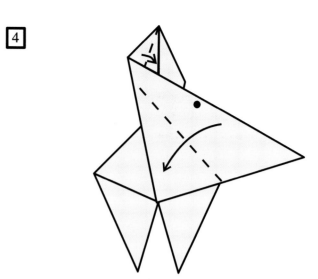

4 Pull the long upper edge of the near flap downward along the existing crease as shown. At the same time bring the short upper left edge to the centerline. Flatten the model. Watch the black dot.

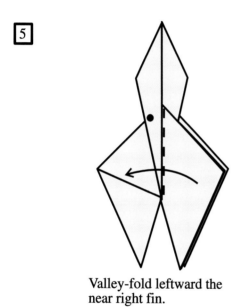

5 Valley-fold leftward the near right fin.

6 Grasp opposite fins and inflate the rocket by blowing into the hole in the bottom.

!!!   CAUTION   !!!
DON'T POKE YOUR EYE!

7

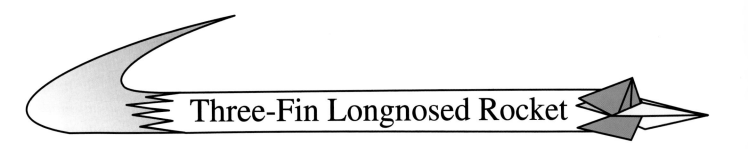

Three-Fin Longnosed Rocket

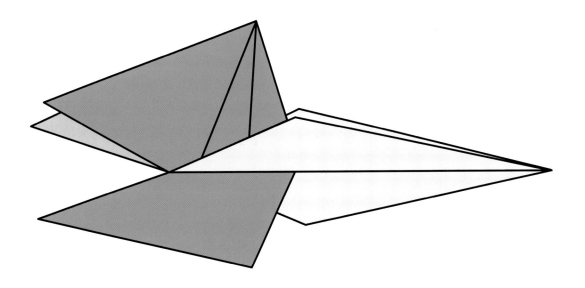

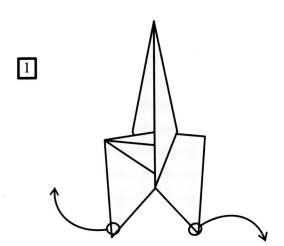

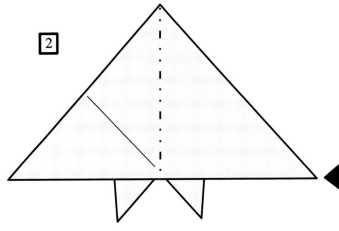

1

Begin with an uninflated Longnosed Rocket (page 13). Grasp the tips of the nearest fins; twist the left fin gently toward the back, and twist the right fin gently in the opposite direction to begin the complete unfolding of the flaps. Assist this unfolding until the flaps have become the front half of a Waterbomb Base.

2

Reverse-fold the near right flap all the way inside the near left flap.

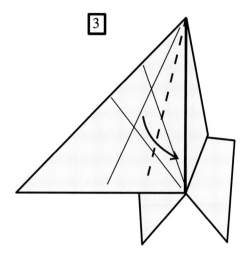

3

Valley-fold the entire left flap
rightward along an existing crease
as shown.

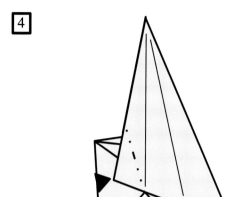

4

Reverse-fold into the model the lower
left corner of the near flap, as shown.
The creases already exist.

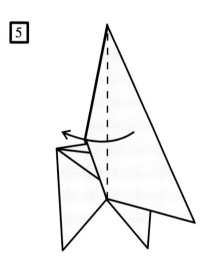

5

Valley-fold the near flap leftward
along the centerline.

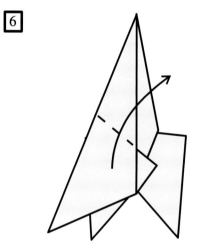

6

Valley-fold the bottom of the near
flap upward along an existing crease.

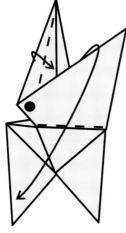

Valley-fold the long upper near edge
downward along the internal folded edge.
At the same time, bring the far left edge
to the centerline. Flatten the model.
Watch the black dot.

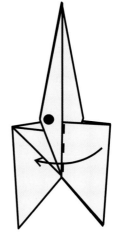

Valley-fold the near right fin
leftward along the centerline.

Grasp opposite fins and inflate the rocket
by blowing into the hole in the bottom.

!!! CAUTION !!!
DON'T POKE YOUR EYE!

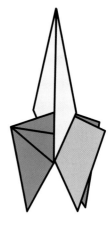

Three-Fin Supersonic Rocket

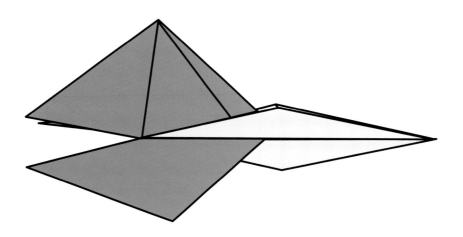

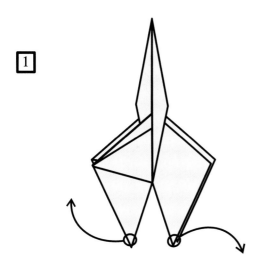

1

Begin with an uninflated Supersonic Rocket (page 17). Grasp the tips of the nearest fins; twist the left fin gently toward the back, and twist the right fin gently in the opposite direction to begin the complete unfolding of the flaps. Assist this unfolding until the flaps have become the front half of a Waterbomb Base.

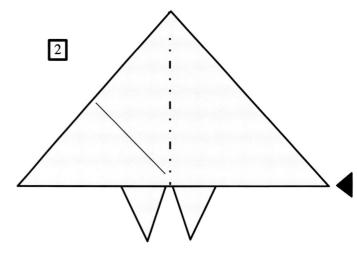

2

Reverse-fold the near right flap all the way inside the near left flap.

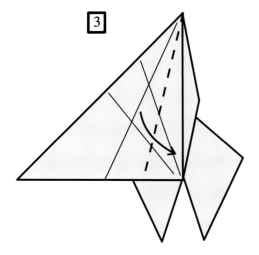

3

Valley-fold the entire left flap
rightward along an existing crease
as shown.

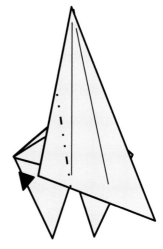

4

Reverse-fold into the model the lower
left corner of the near flap, as shown.
The creases already exist.

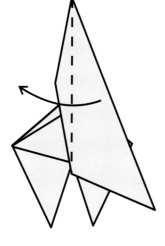

5

Valley-fold the near flap leftward
along the centerline.

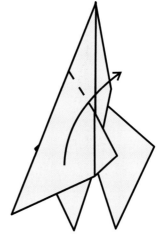

6

Valley-fold the bottom of
the near flap upward along
an existing crease.

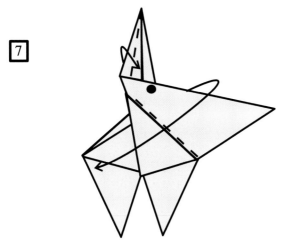

Valley-fold the long upper near edge
downward along the internal folded edge.
At the same time, bring the far left edge
to the centerline. Flatten the model.
Watch the black dot.

8

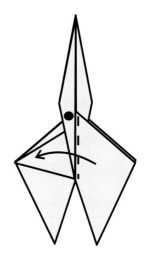

Valley-fold the near right fin
leftward along the centerline.

9

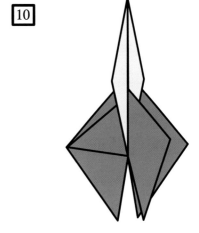

Grasp opposite fins and inflate the rocket
by blowing into the hole in the bottom.

!!! CAUTION !!!
DON'T POKE YOUR EYE!

10

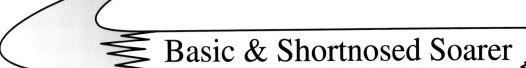 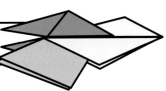

Basic & Shortnosed Soarer

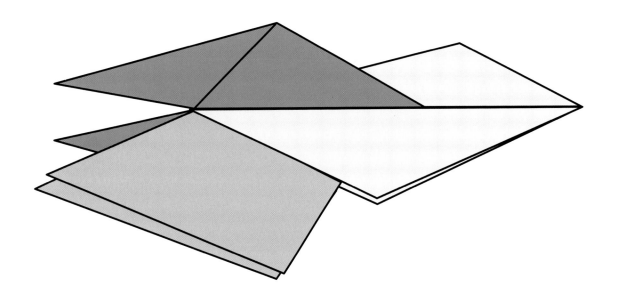

1

Begin with an uninflated Basic Rocket (page 9). Return the near left flap back over the centerline.

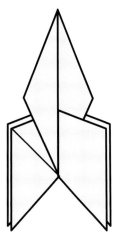

2

Proceed through Step 5 of the Basic Soarer (page 103).

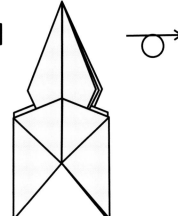

3

Turn the model over.

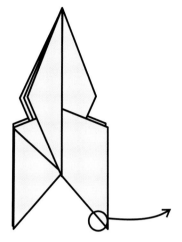

Grasp the tip of the nearest fin
and pull it all the way to the right,
opening the flap completely.

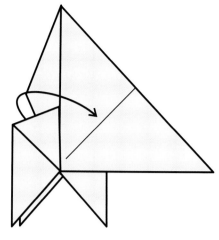

Swing the near fin to the right.

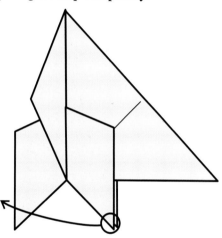

Grasp the tip of the nearest fin
and pull it all the way to the left,
opening the flap completely.

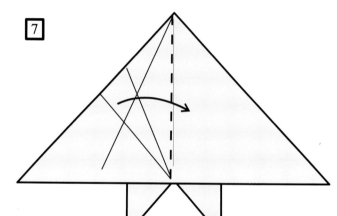

Valley-fold the near left flap
all the way to the right.

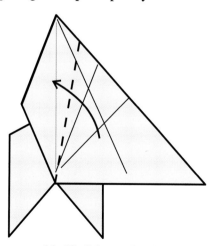

Begin in the shortnosed half of the rocket by
valley-folding the near right flap leftward so that
the crease formed in step 5 of the Rocket Base
lies along the vertical centerline.

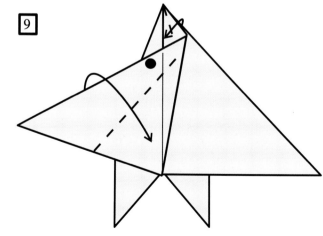

Pull the long upper edge of the near flap downward along
an existing crease; at the same time, bring the short upper
right edge to the centerline. Flatten the model. Watch the
black dot.

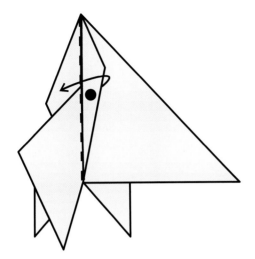

Valley-fold to the left that part
of the slim shortnosed fuselage
just formed.

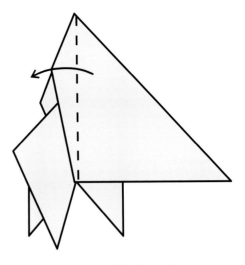

Swing the near right flap all
the way to the left.

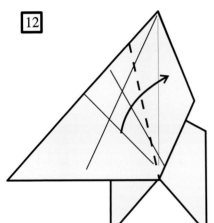

Continue the shortnosed half of the rocket by
valley-folding the near flap rightward so that the crease
formed in step 5 of the Rocket Base lies along the
vertical centerline.

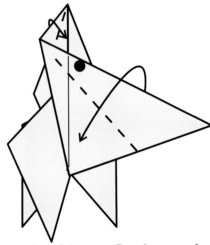

Pull the long upper edge of the near flap downward
along an existing crease; at the same time, bring the
short upper left edge to the centerline. Flatten the
model. Watch the black dot.

Swing to the right the near left part of the fuselage.

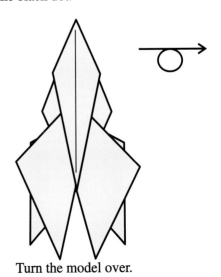

Turn the model over.

16

Pinch the two near fins together
to form a keel.

17

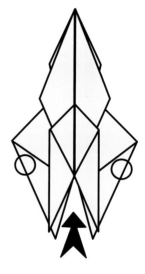

Grasp the two opposite fins and inflate the
rocket by blowing into the hole in the bottom.

!!! CAUTION !!!
DON'T POKE YOUR EYE!

18

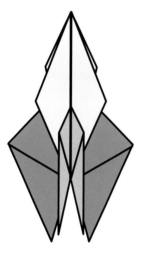

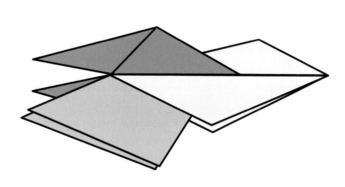

In flight the keel will be nearest to the ground–
we are looking at the underside of the soarer.

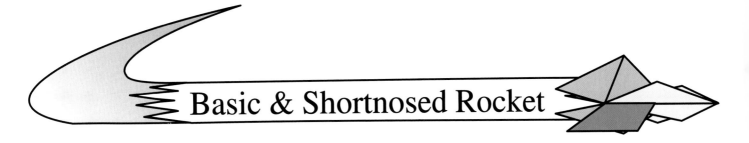

Basic & Shortnosed Rocket

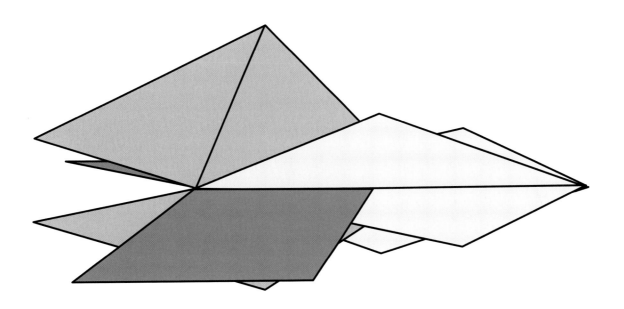

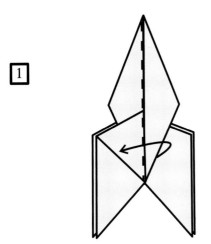

1

Begin with an uninflated Basic Rocket (page 9). Swing the nearest segment of the fuselage leftward along the centerline.

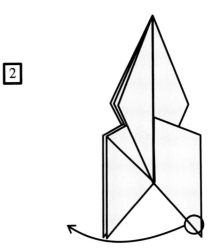

2

Grasp the tip of the near right fin and pull it all the way to the left, opening the flap completely.

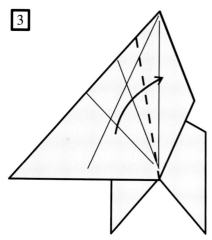

3

Begin the shortnosed half of the rocket by valley-folding the near left flap rightward so that the crease formed in step 5 of the Rocket Base lies along the vertical centerline.

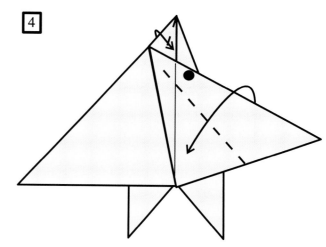

4

Pull the long upper edge of the near flap downward along an existing crease; at the same time, bring the short upper left edge to the centerline. Flatten the model. Watch the black dot.

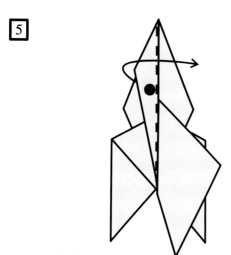

5

Swing the nearest segment of the fuselage rightward along the centerline.

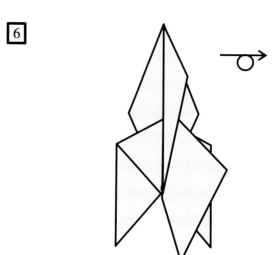

6

Turn the model over.

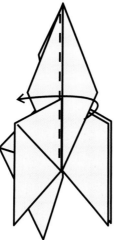

7

Swing the nearest segment of the fuselage leftward along the centerline.

8

Grasp the tip of the near right fin and pull it all the way to the left, opening the flap completely.

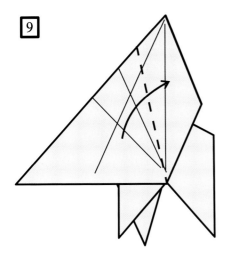

9

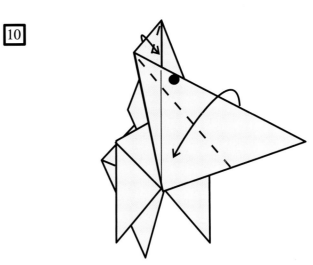

10

Continue the shortnosed half of the rocket by valley-folding the near flap rightward so that the crease formed in step 5 of the Rocket Base lies along the vertical centerline.

Pull the long upper edge of the near flap downward along an existing crease; at the same time, bring the short upper left edge to the centerline. Flatten the model. Watch the black dot.

11

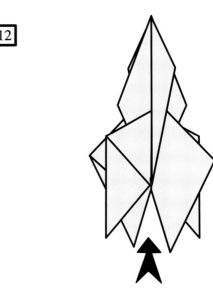

12

Swing the nearest segment of the fuselage rightward along the centerline.

Grasp opposite fins and inflate the rocket by blowing into the hole in the bottom.

!!!   CAUTION   !!!
DON'T POKE YOUR EYE!

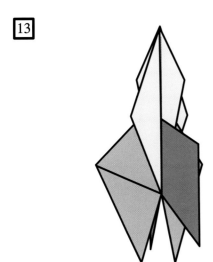

13

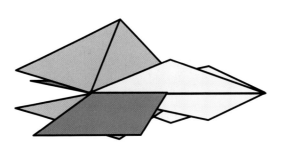

Shortnosed Spinner

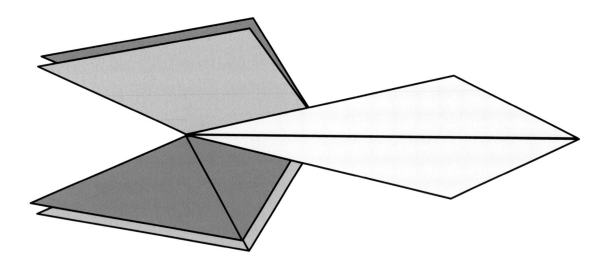

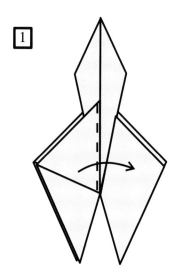

Begin with an uninflated Shortnosed Rocket (page 11). Return the near left flap back over the centerline.

Valley-fold the near fin leftward–the crease is even with the edge of the fuselage. Unfold.

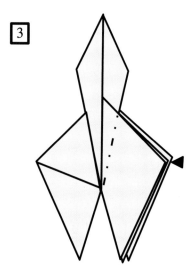

Reverse-fold the fin into itself along the crease formed in step 1. The flap will emerge at the left.

4

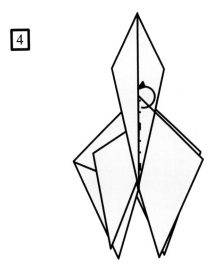

Mountain-fold the small flap formed in step 3,
tucking it into the model under all possible flaps.

5

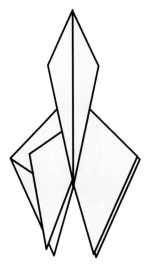

Repeat steps 1–4 on the
three remaining fins.

6

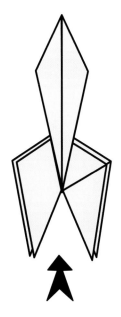

Grasp opposite fins and inflate the rocket
by blowing into the hole in the bottom.

!!! CAUTION !!!
DON'T POKE YOUR EYE!

7

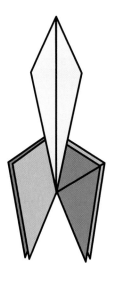

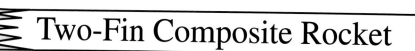

Two-Fin Composite Rocket

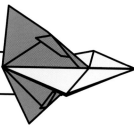

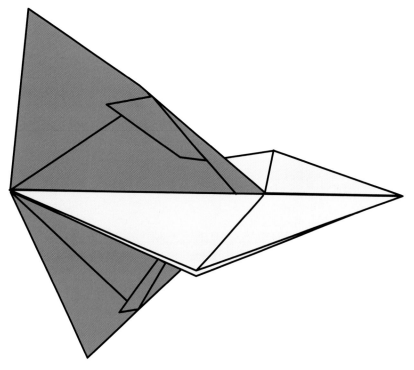

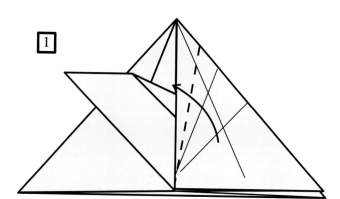

1 Begin with the Basic Winged Rocket (page 23). Unfold three flaps so that the model looks like this. Then valley-fold the near right flap leftward so that the existing crease lies along the vertical centerline.

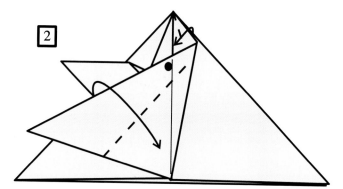

2 Pull the long upper edge of the near flap downward along the existing crease; at the same time, bring the short upper right edge to the centerline. Watch the black dot. Flatten the model.

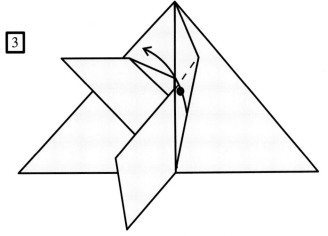

3

Lift the nearest fin up and flatten it to the left as far as it will go.

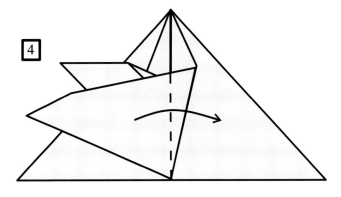

4

Swing the near flap rightward along the centerline.

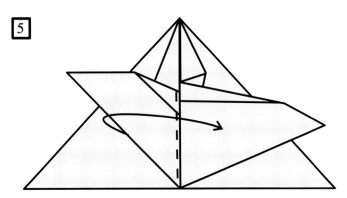

5

Swing the near left flap all the way to the right.

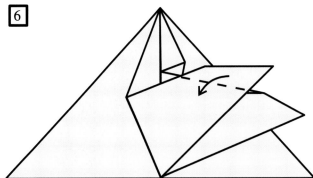

6

Valley-fold the upper edge of the near right flap down so that it is even with the upper edge of the flap behind it.

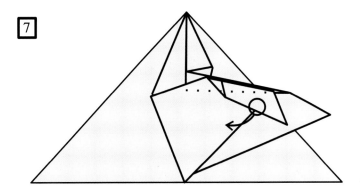

7

Grasp the near wing and pull it gently clockwise.

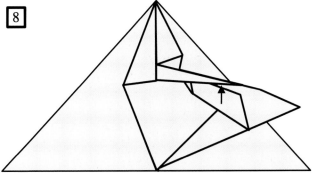

8

Tuck the upper edge of the near wing into the narrow horizontal pocket that lies along the upper edge of the large wing behind it. To do this neatly it will be necessary to loosen the pocket slightly near the vertical centerline, and then to refold the pocket and the near wing as one.

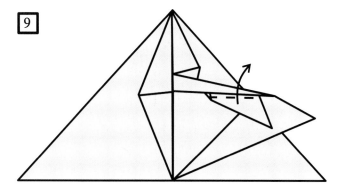

9

Valley-fold the small triangular flap up.

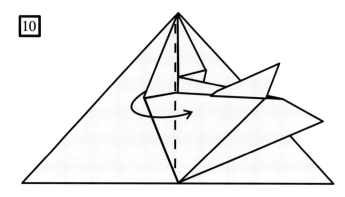

10

Swing the near left segment of the fuselage all the way to the right.

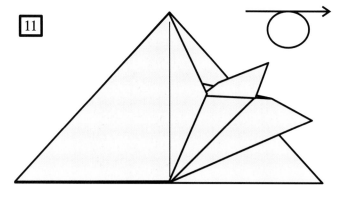

11

Turn the model over.

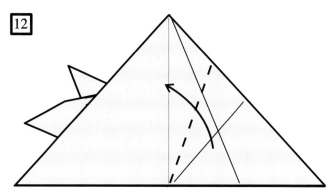

12

Valley-fold the near right flap leftward along the existing crease.

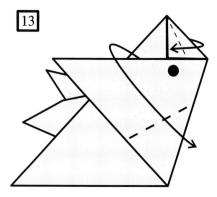

13

Pull the long upper edge of the near flap downward along the existing crease; at the same time, bring the short upper right edge to the centerline. Watch the black dot. Flatten the model.

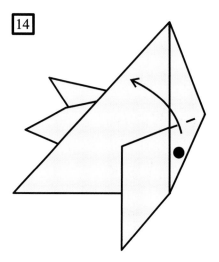

14

Valley-fold the near flap upward as far as it will go.

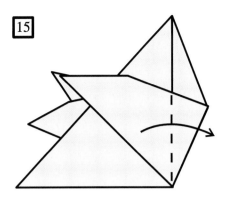

15

Valley-fold the near flap rightward along the centerline.

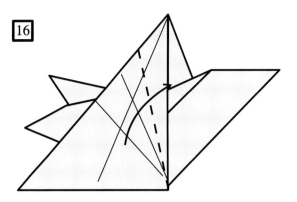

16

Valley-fold the near flap rightward so that the existing crease lies along the vertical centerline.

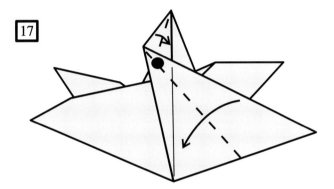

17

Pull the long upper edge of the near flap downward; at the same time, bring the short upper left edge to the centerline. Watch the black dot. Flatten the model.

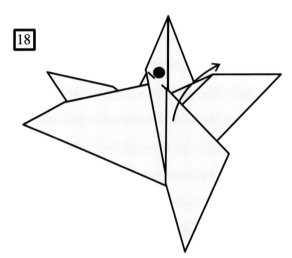

18

Lift the near right flap and flatten it rightward as far as it will go.

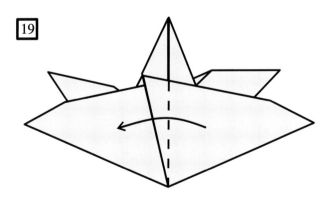

19

Valley-fold the near flap leftward along the centerline.

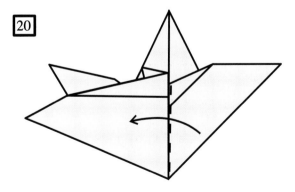

20

Swing the near right wing all the way to the left.

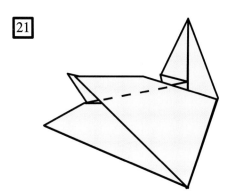

21

Valley-fold the upper edge of the near wing
down so that it is even with the upper edge
of the wing behind it.

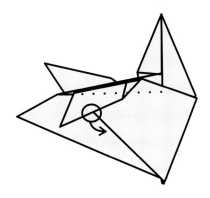

22

Grasp the near wing and pull
it gently counterclockwise.

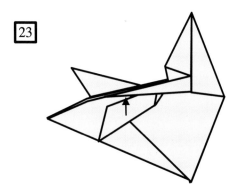

23

Tuck the upper edge of the near wing into the narrow
horizontal pocket that lies along the upper edge of the
large wing behind it. To do this neatly it will be
necessary to loosen the pocket slightly near the vertical
centerline, and then to refold the pocket and the near
wing as one.

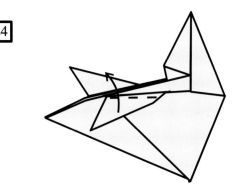

24

Valley-fold the small triangular flap up.

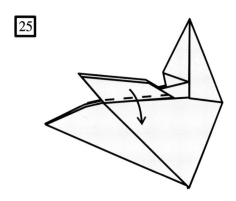

25

Swing the small triangular flap downward again–it will
stand out at an angle from the wing as a whole.
Repeat behind.

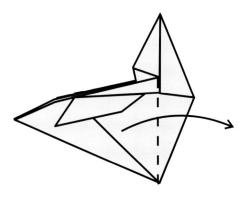

26

Swing the near wing all the way to the right.

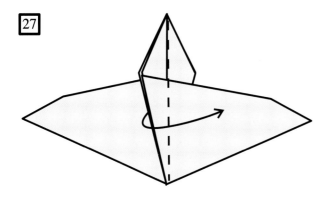

27

Valley-fold the near segment of the fuselage
rightward over the centerline.

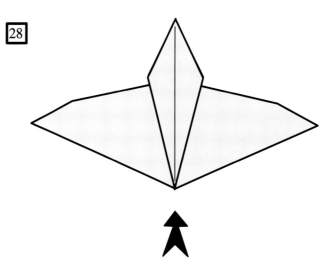

28

Grasp opposite fins and inflate the rocket
by blowing into the hole in the bottom.

!!!   CAUTION   !!!
DON'T POKE YOUR EYE!

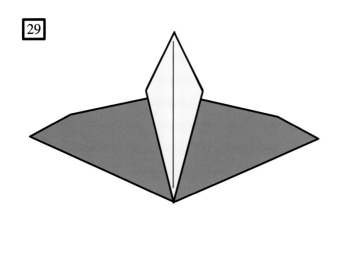

29

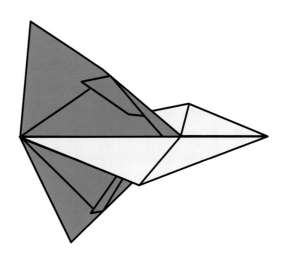

Rocket Design: Nose & Fuselage

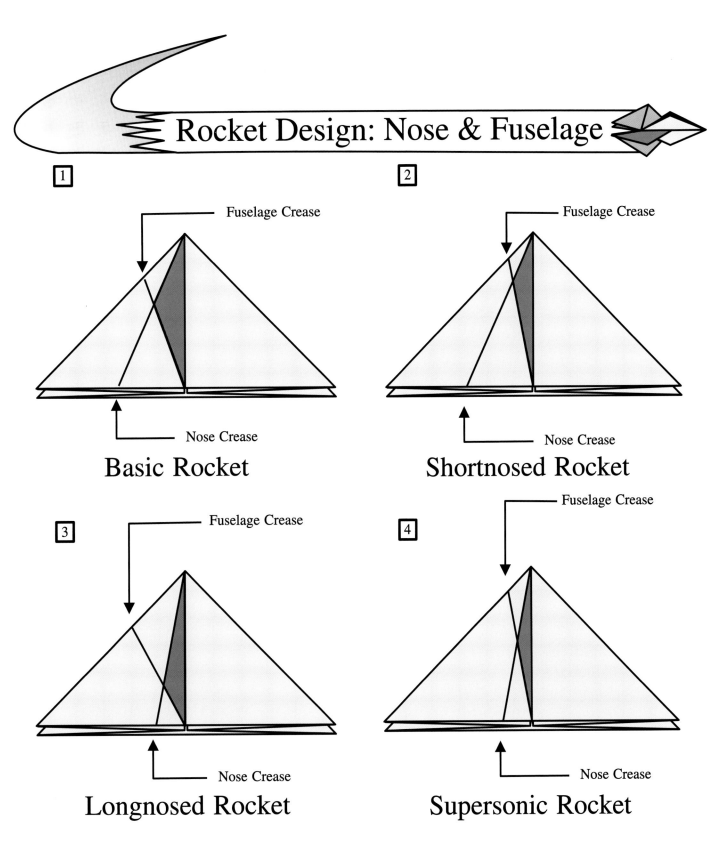

1

Fuselage Crease

Nose Crease

Basic Rocket

2

Fuselage Crease

Nose Crease

Shortnosed Rocket

3

Fuselage Crease

Nose Crease

Longnosed Rocket

4

Fuselage Crease

Nose Crease

Supersonic Rocket

The drawings above show the location of the creases used to form the rockets. Each of the four rockets is formed by changing the location of the fuselage and nose creases. The Basic Rocket shown in drawing 1, has a large nose and wide fuselage because the creases are located away from the centerline of the Waterbomb Base. As the location of these creases change so do the proportions of the rocket. The shaded areas of the four drawings show the shape of the rocket as the creases change.

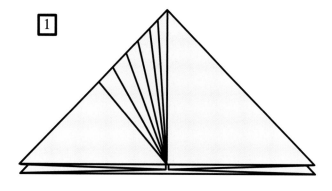

Fuselage Creases

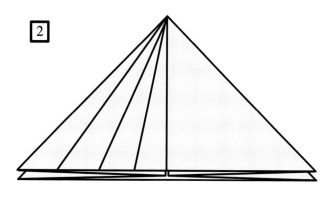

Nose Creases

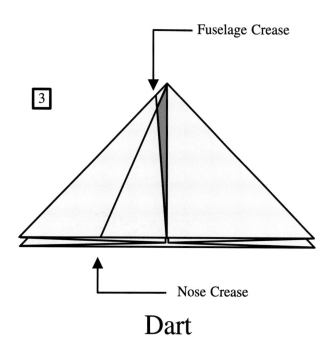

Fuselage Crease

Nose Crease

Dart

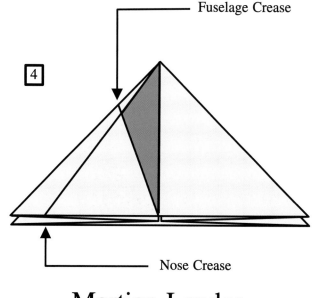

Fuselage Crease

Nose Crease

Martian Lander

You can adjust the size of the fuselage by changing the location of the crease shown in drawing 1. The closer the crease is to the centerline of the Waterbomb Base, the smaller the fuselage becomes.

You can adjust the size of the nose by changing the location of the crease shown in drawing 2. The closer the crease is to the centerline of the Waterbomb Base, the narrower and smaller the nose becomes.

The last two rockets found in this book are shown in drawings 3 and 4. Drawing 3 shows the Dart. It will have a very small and short nose and a very narrow fuselage. Drawing 4 shows the location of the fuselage and nose crease lines used to form the Martian Lander. It will have a broad nose and a wide fuselage.

Rocket Design: Fins

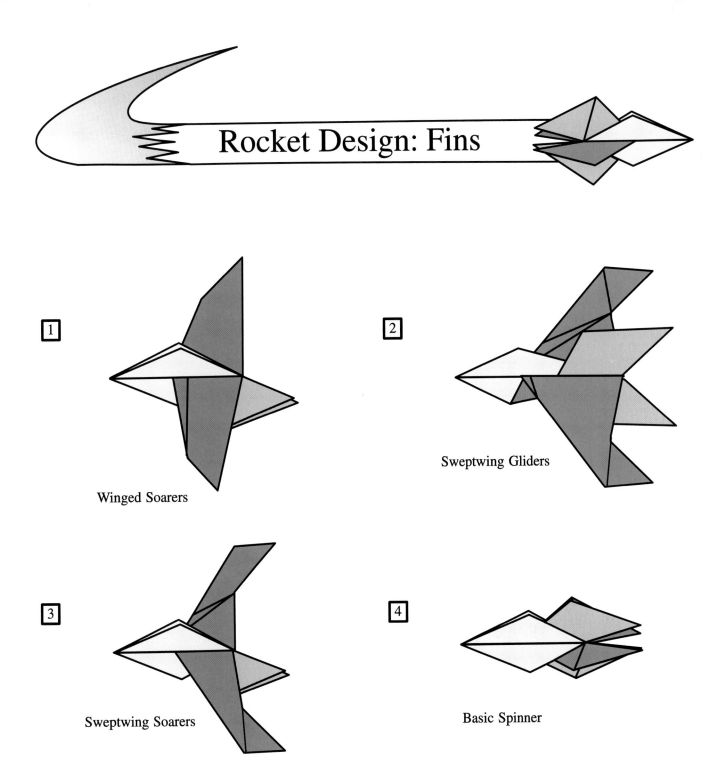

1   Winged Soarers

2   Sweptwing Gliders

3   Sweptwing Soarers

4   Basic Spinner

There are many different combinations of rocket fins—far too many to show how to fold every one. Now that you know how to fold the various fins shown in this book, try folding different rockets with different configurations. The drawings on this page show some possible combinations. You can fold, create and name your own rockets using the instructions in this book. You are limited only by your imagination in creating your own rockets and seeing how they fly.

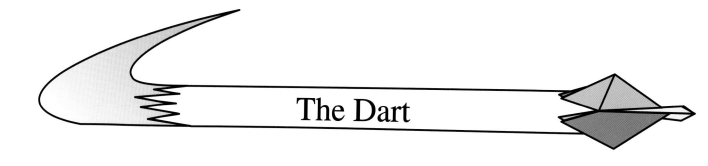

The Dart

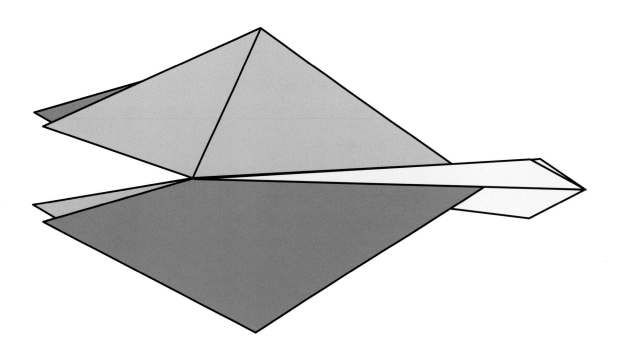

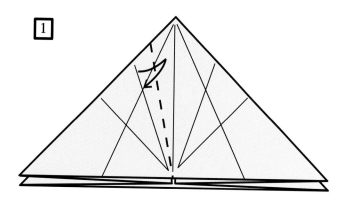

1

Begin with a Rocket Base (page 6).
Valley fold the crease made in step 5
over to the vertical centerline and unfold.

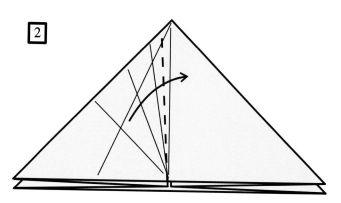

2

Valley-fold the crease formed in step 1
over to the centerline.

3

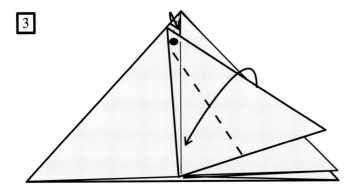

Pull the long upper edge of the near flap downward.
The crease already exists, but it must be turned into a
valley fold. At the same time bring the short upper left
edge to the vertical centerline. Watch the black dot.

4

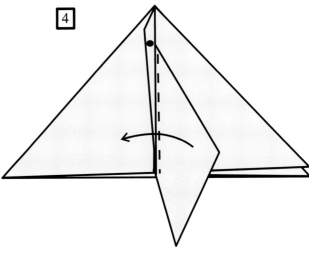

Valley-fold leftward the right part
of the near flap to form a large fin. Repeat
steps 1–4 on the remaining three flaps.

5

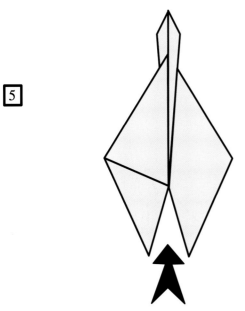

Grasp opposite fins and inflate the rocket
by blowing into the hole in the bottom.

!!!   CAUTION   !!!
DON'T POKE YOUR EYE!

6

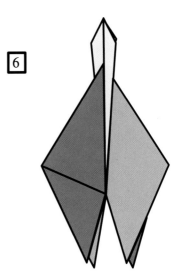

Lunar Lander

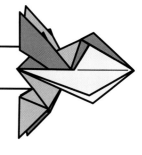

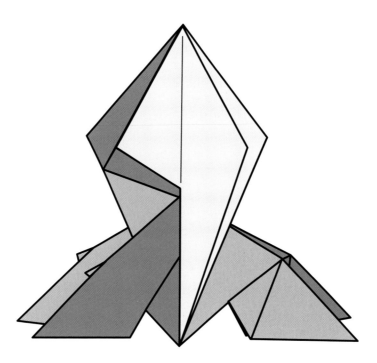

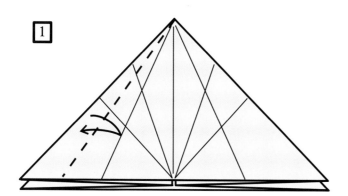

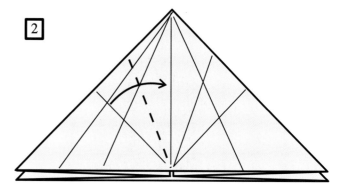

Begin with a Rocket Base (page 6).
Valley-fold the edge of the near
left flap over to the crease made in
step 1 of the Rocket Base and unfold.

Valley-fold the near left flap along the existing
crease formed in step 5 of the Rocket Base.

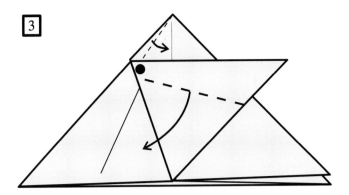

3

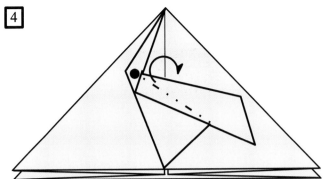

4

Pull the long upper edge of the near flap downward. The crease was formed in step 1 of the Lunar Lander, but it must be turned into a valley fold. At the same time bring the short upper left edge toward the right. Flatten the model. Watch the black dot.

Mountain-fold the top edge of the inner flap down inside the near flap as shown to form a lander fin. The mountain crease extends all the way in to the left corner. The foot should lie along the horizontal lower edge of the base. See step 5.

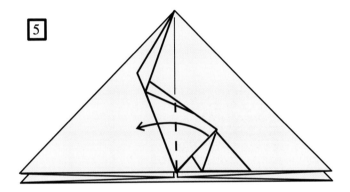

5

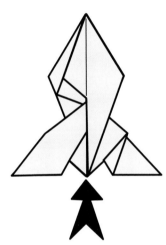

6

Valley-fold the right half of the near flap over the centerline to form a fin. Repeat steps 1–5 on the three remaining sides.

Grasp opposite fins and inflate the rocket by blowing into the hole in the bottom.

!!! CAUTION !!!
DON'T POKE YOUR EYE!

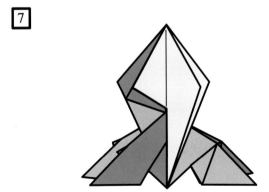

7

Rocket Nose Cone

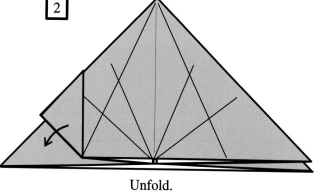

1

Begin with a square of paper one-fourth the area of the Rocket Base. If the Rocket Base is folded from an eight-inch square, use a four-inch square for the Nose Cone. Fold this square into a small Rocket Base. Valley-fold the near left corner as shown; the crease is at a right angle to the folded edge.

2

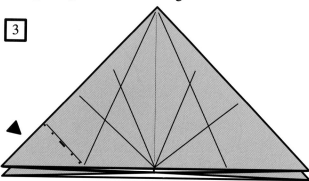

Unfold.

3

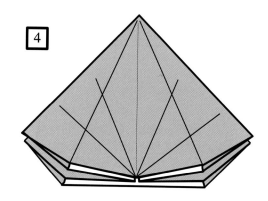

Reverse-fold the corner inward using the existing crease. Repeat steps 1–3 on the three remaining flaps.

4

5

Place the Nose Cone (shown here in greatly reduced size) on the Rocket Base prior to folding a rocket. The inner edges of the Nose Cone should slide into the grooves between the front and back layers of the Rocket Base.

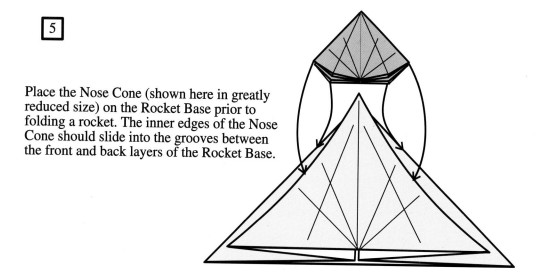

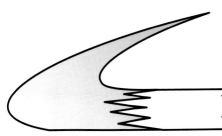

Escape Capsule

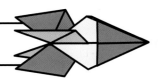

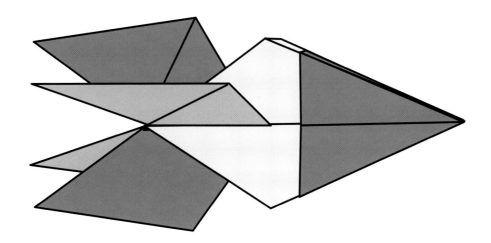

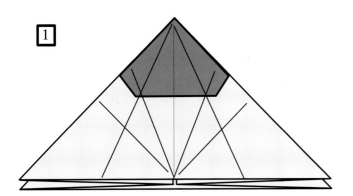

1

Begin by placing a Nose Cone onto
a Rocket Base.

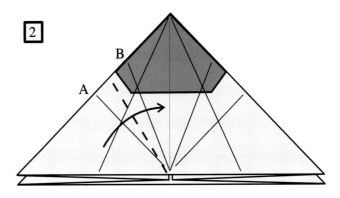

2

B

A

Valley-fold the near left flap so that
crease A lies on Crease B.

The Escape Capsule will allow you to practice folding a rocket with a Nose Cone. The Nose Cone is folded right along with the rocket and will become an integral part of the model as you fold.

3

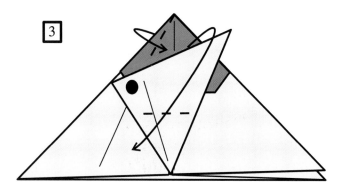

Pull the long upper edge of the near flap downward along the existing crease as shown. At the same time bring the short upper left edge to the centerline. Flatten the model. Watch the black dot.

4

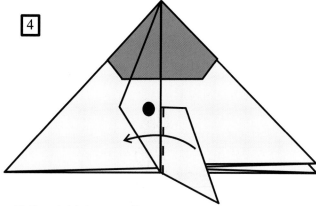

Valley-fold the near fin to the left along the centerline. Repeat steps 2-4 on the three remaining flaps.

5

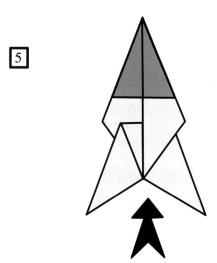

Grasp opposite fins an inflate the rocket by blowing into the hole in the bottom.

!!! CAUTION !!!
DON'T POKE YOUR EYE!

6

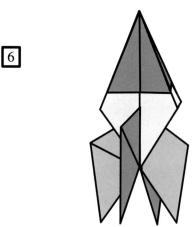

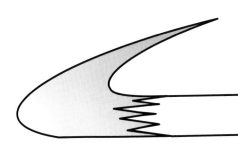 # Flying Rockets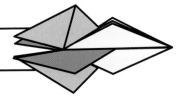

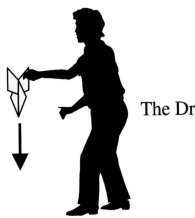

The Drop

The drop requires only that the model be dropped from a certain height. The Floaters will fly best using the drop or the lift because of their open fins. These fins catch the air and will not work best if you try to throw them hard.

The Toss

The toss requires a little arm movement to send the model on its way. The Winged Rockets and Soarers will fly best using the toss or drop because of their large wide fins. These fins will allow the model to glide gently through the air. They will not work well if you throw them because the rocket resists forward motion.

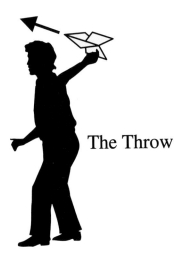

The Throw

The throw requires a great deal of arm movement to propel the model. Rockets, Sweptwings, Landers, and Zoomers fly best when they are thrown into the air. The fins allow the rocket to fly faster with little air resistance.

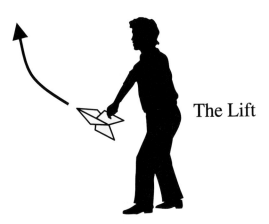

The Lift

The lift requires that the model be thrown upward. The Gliders will fly best using the lift because they have both simple rocket fins and winged fins. These rockets need a little extra height to fly well but there is still too much air resistance to use a hard throw.

The rockets require different means of propulsion. If you add the Nose Cone to any of the models they will fly higher and farther with gentle arm movements.

There are many sources of rockets you can find to enlarge your fleet. Here are a few of the many books containing rockets and jets you can fold. Information on origami and paper folding can be found through the Origami OUSA.

Origami in Action: Paper Toys that Fly, Flap, Gobble, and Inflate!
copyright 1997 by Robert J. Lang
St. Martin's Griffin

Planes, Jets, & Helicopters: Great Paper Airplanes
copyright 1994 by John Bringhurst
Tab Books

How to Make Origami Airplanes That Fly
copyright 1992 by Gery Hsu
Dover Publications

Wings & Things: Origami That Flies
copyright 1989 by Stephen Weiss
St. Martin's Press

Information on origami and paper folding can be found through Origami USA.

OrigamiUSA
15 West 77th Street
New York, NY 10024-5192
USA
tel (212) 769-5635
fax (212) 769-5668

OrigamiUSA formerly The Friends of The Origami Center of America is a not-for-profit, tax-exempt, educational and cultural arts organization which is dedicated to the sharing of paperfolding in America and around the world. There are over 2000 members in 49 states and 19 countries and there are affiliate groups in cities all over the United States and Canada.

OrigamiUSA is headquartered autonomously in New York City's American Museum of Natural History through the generosity of the Museum Trustees. It is staffed primarily by volunteers and maintains the largest origami library in the world, as well as hundreds of diagrams of unpublished models.

OrigamiUSA holds classes, workshops and an annual convention. It publishes a quarterly magazine, instruction booklets and the Annual Collection (a 300 page compilation of original models), and maintains a lending library which is available to OrigamiUSA members.

OrigamiUSA is an excellent source for origami books and supplies. Its mail-order-only supply center, The Origami Source, located at another address, sells a tremendous variety of origami books, papers, and videos.

Your public library will have a collection of origami books.